Printed in the United States of America
by G&R Publishing Co.

Distributed By:

Products

507 Industrial Street
Waverly, IA 50677

ISBN 1-56383-167-8
Item # 7001

Table of Contents

Tips on Freezing

* To ensure food safety, it is best to freeze foods as quickly as possible. Place hot foods directly in the refrigerator or freezer to cool, rather than let sit at room temperature.

* Rapid change in temperature can break some glass dishes. Do not put a frozen glass dish directly into a hot oven. Also, do not put a hot glass dish into cold water or a freezer.

* When freezing food in a casserole dish, cover with a layer of plastic wrap first then top with a lid or layer of tin foil. This helps prevent moisture loss and freezer burn.

* Label all containers and freezer bags with the name of the recipe, the date they were first placed in the freezer and how long they can remain frozen. For example: Manhattan Clam Chowder, January 1, 2004, Good until April 1, 2004.

* Do not overload your freezer with unfrozen foods. Add only the amount that will freeze within 24 hours, which is usually 2 to 3 pounds of food per cubic foot of storage space. Too many unfrozen foods slows down the freezing rate and may result in loss of quality.

* Leave a little space between packages so air can circulate freely. Once the food has frozen, the packages may be stored closer together.

* If you experience a power outage, leave the freezer door shut. Food usually remains safe for up to 48 hours if the door is not repeatedly opened.

Tips on Thawing & Reheating

* Do not thaw food at room temperature. Foods can be safely defrosted in the refrigerator, under cold running water or in the microwave.

* To save space, store recipes that do not require a specific mold or shape (such as soups and sauces) in freezer bags.

* Do not refreeze unused portions of previously frozen, reheated meals. Use the unused portion within 1 to 2 days in the leftover state.

* Foods should be heated until bubbly throughout or to an internal temperature of 145° to 165° F. Soups, gravies and stews should be heated to a simmer for 1 to 2 minutes.

* Never leave foods, raw or cooked, at room temperature longer than 2 hours. On a hot day with temperatures at 90° F or warmer, this decreases to 1 hour.

Veggies & Sides

Apple Sauce

Makes 4 to 5 cups

4 lbs. apples, washed, cored and quartered
1 C. water or apple juice

1 T. fresh lemon juice
1/2 C. sugar or honey

Cut apples into 1/2" slices. Be sure to peel apples if mashing them by hand. If using a sieve, food processor or blender, peels can be left on apples. In a large, heavy saucepan, simmer apples in water or apple juice over low heat until tender but not mushy. Add lemon juice. Stir in sugar or honey. Cook and stir until the sweetener dissolves. Depending on the tartness of the apples, the amount of sweetener may be adjusted. Remove from heat and allow to cool slightly before mashing. Transfer to a freezer bag to freeze.

Variations

May add 1 teaspoon cinnamon and 1/2 teaspoon nutmeg. May substitute 3 cups cranberries or blueberries for 1 pound of the apples. May substitute peaches, pears, plums or apricots for half of the apples.

To prepare

Thaw apple sauce and serve chilled or warmed over stovetop.

FREEZE
up to 9 months.

2

Winter Squash with Honey, Cranberries & Walnuts

Makes 4 to 6 servings

1 egg	3/4 C. cranberries, fresh or frozen
1/4 C. butter, melted	1/4 C. frozen orange juice
3 C. mashed winter squash	concentrate
(use butternut, Hubbard	1/8 C. honey
or buttercup)*	1/2 C. chopped walnuts

In a medium bowl, lightly beat egg. Stir in melted butter and mashed squash. In a separate bowl, combine cranberries, frozen orange juice, honey and chopped walnuts, creating a cranberry mixture. Add 1/4 of the cranberry mixture to the squash mixture. Spoon squash mixture into a greased 1-quart casserole dish. Top with remaining cranberry mixture. Cover and freeze.

* To make mashed squash, use one medium winter squash. Roast in halves, face down and scoop out meat to puree. Or, peel squash, cut into cubes and simmer until tender before mashing.

To prepare

Preheat oven to 350°. Bake frozen squash, loosely covered, for approximately 1 hour.

FREEZE
up to 6 months.

3

Ratatouille or Stewed Summer Vegetables

Makes 1 1/2 to 2 quarts

1 large (about 1 lb.) eggplant, peeled and cut into 1" cubes	2 large red bell peppers, cut into 1" squares
2 medium zucchini, cut into 1" cubes	3 cloves garlic, minced
1/4 C. plus 2 T. olive oil, divided	2 medium fresh tomatoes, chopped
1 1/2 C. sliced onions	1 tsp. dried thyme
	Salt & pepper to taste

In a skillet, sauté eggplant and zucchini in 1/4 cup olive oil over high heat for 8 to 10 minutes or until vegetables are almost tender. Remove to a lightly greased 2-quart casserole dish. Keeping the skillet hot, add remaining 2 tablespoons olive oil, onions, peppers and garlic. Cook, stirring occasionally, for 10 minutes or until peppers are just tender. Add tomatoes, thyme, salt and pepper. Stir to combine. Pour into the casserole dish, covering the eggplant mixture. Cover and freeze.

To prepare

Shredded mozzarella cheese   **Fresh chopped basil**

Preheat oven to 375°. Cover and bake frozen vegetables for 30 minutes. Uncover and bake an additional 40 minutes. If desired, top with mozzarella cheese for final 10 minutes or season with fresh chopped basil.

FREEZE
up to 9 months.

Stuffed Bell Peppers

Makes 4 stuffed peppers

3/4 lb. ground beef or pork	3/4 tsp. dried basil
1/2 medium onion, finely diced	Salt & pepper to taste
1 1/2 tsp. minced garlic	4 bell peppers, any color
1 C. cooked rice	1/2 C. bread crumbs
2 eggs, lightly beaten	1 T. butter, melted
1/2 tsp. dried thyme	1 1/2 tsp. dried parsley
1 tsp. paprika	

In a medium skillet, brown meat, adding a touch of vegetable oil. Cook until fully browned, stirring occasionally to break up the meat. Drain the fat, add onions and garlic and cook until just tender but not browned. Remove from heat and add rice, eggs, thyme, paprika, basil, salt and pepper. Stir together and set aside. Cut the top 1/2" from each bell pepper and remove the seeds from the inside. If necessary, cut a bit off the bottoms so the peppers will stand upright in a baking dish. Stuff each pepper with the meat and rice stuffing. In a small bowl, mix bread crumbs, melted butter and parsley. Top each pepper with bread crumb mixture. Cover and freeze.

To prepare

Preheat oven to 375°. Bake the frozen peppers in a baking dish or on a baking sheet for 45 to 55 minutes.

FREEZE
up to 6 months
(3 months if using frozen meat.)

5

Bean & Cheddar Casserole

Makes 1 1/2 quarts (4 to 6 servings)

3 slices bacon, diced
1 medium onion, diced
1 T. chopped garlic
1 1/2 tsp. chili powder
4 C. cooked beans (kidney,
    pinto or red beans)

1 (28 oz.) can tomatoes, drained
    and coarsely chopped
Salt & pepper to taste
1 1/4 C. shredded Cheddar cheese,
    divided

In a hot skillet, cook bacon until only a little fat remains. Add the onions and garlic and cook until the onions are tender and the bacon is slightly browned, approximately 10 to 12 minutes. Add chili powder, cooked beans, drained tomatoes, salt and pepper. Stir together and pour half of the bean mixture into a greased 2-quart casserole dish. Top with half of the cheese. Repeat with the remaining beans and cheese. Cover and freeze.

To prepare

Preheat oven to 350°. Cover and bake frozen casserole for 25 minutes. Uncover and bake an additional 25 to 30 minutes.

FREEZE
up to 6 months.

Garlic Mashed Potatoes

Makes 8 servings

5 lbs. Yukon Gold potatoes	**4 oz. cream cheese**
1 small pkg. Hidden Valley	**1 tsp. garlic powder**
ranch dressing mix	**1 C. milk, whole or 2%**

Peel potatoes and cut into 2" chunks. Place in a 5 to 6-quart pan. Add water to cover potatoes and bring to a boil over high heat. Reduce heat to low. Simmer until the potatoes are very tender, about 20 to 25 minutes. Drain water and return potatoes to the pan. Add ranch dressing mix, cream cheese, garlic powder and milk. Mash potatoes with a potato masher or wooden spoon, depending on the texture you desire. In refrigerator, allow potatoes to cool to room temperature. Divide potatoes into greased 8" to 9" oven-safe casserole dishes. Cover with foil and freeze.

To prepare

Preheat oven to 375°. If potatoes are thawed, cover casserole dishes and heat for 40 minutes. If heating frozen potatoes, cover casserole dishes and heat for 90 minutes.

FREEZE
up to 6 months.

Freezer Coleslaw

10 C. (1 medium head) shredded
   cabbage
1 carrot, shredded
1 green pepper, finely chopped
1 tsp. salt

1 C. vinegar
2 C. sugar
1 tsp. celery seeds
1 tsp. mustard

In a large bowl, combine shredded cabbage, carrots, green peppers and salt. Let stand for 1 hour. In a medium saucepan over medium heat, combine vinegar, sugar, celery seeds and mustard and bring to a boil. Boil for 1 minute and let cool. Drain cabbage mixture of water and stir in vinegar mixture. Stir gently. Freeze in tightly-sealed freezer bags or containers.

To prepare

Thaw coleslaw and serve chilled.

FREEZE
up to 6 months.

8

Marinara Sauce

3 T. olive oil
2 T. chopped garlic
1 medium onion, diced
2 medium carrots, diced
1 (28 oz.) can whole tomatoes
    in juice, coarsely chopped

1 T. dried basil
1 tsp. dried oregano
2 tsp. sugar
1/2 tsp. red pepper flakes
Salt & pepper to taste

In a medium to large saucepan, heat olive oil. Cook garlic, onions and carrots until just softened, stirring occasionally. Stir in tomatoes with juice, basil, oregano, sugar, red pepper flakes, salt and pepper. Bring to a boil and simmer for 15 to 20 minutes. Transfer to a freezer bag to freeze. For easy preparation, freeze marinara sauce in quantities needed for other recipes.

To prepare

Thaw and use in recipes as needed.

FREEZE
up to 9 months.

9

White Sauce

2 T. cornstarch   **2 C. milk**
1 tsp. salt   **2 T. butter or margarine**
1/4 tsp. pepper

In medium saucepan, combine cornstarch, salt and pepper. Using a wire whisk, stir in milk until smooth. Add butter or margarine. Stirring constantly with a rubber spatula, bring to a boil over medium high heat and boil 1 minute. Remove from heat. Cool white sauce and transfer to a freezer bag to freeze. For easy preparation, freeze white sauce in quantities needed for other recipes.

To prepare

Thaw and use in recipes as needed.

FREEZE
up to 6 months.

Whipped Sweet Potatoes

Makes 2 to 2 1/2 quarts

4 carrots, peeled and cubed	1/4 C. brown sugar
3 lbs. (about 3 medium) sweet potatoes, peeled and cubed	2 T. fresh orange juice
	1 tsp. nutmeg
2 chicken bouillon cubes	Salt and pepper to taste
6 T. butter	

In a stock pot, place peeled and cubed carrots, peeled and cubed sweet potatoes and chicken bouillon cubes and cover with water. Bring to a boil and simmer until vegetables are very tender, approximately 20 to 25 minutes. Drain, leaving 1/3 cup of the cooking liquid. Transfer to a blender, food processor or hand mixer. Add butter, brown sugar, orange juice, nutmeg, salt and pepper. Whip until mixture is light and fluffy. Freeze in freezer bags or casserole dish.

To prepare

Thaw in refrigerator or microwave. Preheat oven to 350°. Cover and bake for 35 to 40 minutes.

FREEZE
up to 6 months.

11

Apple Sweet Potato Stuffing

4 medium sweet potatoes	1/2 C. apple cider
4 T. butter	1/4 tsp. cinnamon
1 medium onion, chopped	1/4 tsp. nutmeg
3 stalks celery, chopped	1/2 tsp. dried thyme
2 C. tart apples, peeled, cored	1 1/2 tsp. dried parsley
and diced	1/2 C. chicken broth, canned or
2 C. unseasoned bread crumbs	prepared with bouillon

In a large pot, roast sweet potatoes whole and unpeeled or boil in water. Allow to cool before peeling and mashing sweet potatoes by hand with a fork. Set aside. In a medium skillet, heat butter and sauté onions and celery until just softened. Add apples and sauté a few minutes more. In a medium mixing bowl, combine onion and apple mixture with sweet potatoes, bread crumbs, apple cider, cinnamon, nutmeg, thyme, parsley and chicken broth. Toss together and transfer to a greased 2-quart casserole dish. Cover and freeze.

To prepare

Thaw in refrigerator or microwave. Preheat oven to 350°. Cover and bake for 45 to 55 minutes.

FREEZE
up to 6 months.

Black Beans & Rice

1 (15 oz.) can black beans, drained
1 (10 oz.) can tomatoes and
   green chilies, drained
1 C. salsa

2 C. cooked rice
1 C. sour cream
2 C. shredded Cheddar cheese,
   divided

In a medium bowl, combine drained black beans, drained tomatoes, salsa, cooked rice, sour cream and 1 cup Cheddar cheese. Mix well. Transfer to a greased 2-quart casserole dish to freeze and top with remaining Cheddar cheese. Cover and freeze.

To prepare

Thaw in refrigerator or microwave. Preheat oven to 350°. Cover and bake for 30 minutes. Remove cover and bake an additional 10 to 15 minutes.

FREEZE
up to 6 months.

Rice Stuffing

1 1/2 T. butter
1 stalk celery, diced
1 small onion, diced
2/3 C. chopped walnuts or
   pecans

1/2 C. raisins or currants
1/2 tsp. paprika
3 C. cooked rice
1/3 C. cooked and crumbled
   bacon

In a medium skillet, melt butter. Sauté celery and onions until tender. Add nuts, raisins, paprika and 1/2 cup water. Simmer for 10 minutes to allow fruit to plump. Remove from heat and stir together with cooked rice and crumbled bacon. Transfer to a casserole dish, cover and freeze.

To prepare

Thaw in refrigerator or microwave. Preheat oven to 350°. Cover and bake for 35 to 45 minutes. Serve as a side dish with roast meat or use to stuff chicken, turkey, pork chops, etc.

FREEZE
up to 6 months.

Western-Style Beans

3/4 lb. pork sausage
1 medium onion, chopped
1 T. minced garlic
2 (15 oz.) cans pinto beans,
　drained
1 (15 oz.) can whole tomatoes,
　drained and coarsely
　chopped

3/4 C. barbecue sauce
1 T. brown sugar
1 T. vinegar
2 tsp. chili powder
1 1/2 tsp. dried mustard
Salt and cayenne pepper to
　taste

In a medium skillet, brown sausage and drain off most of the fat. Add onions and garlic and continue to cook until onions are tender. Remove from heat. Add drained pinto beans, drained chopped tomatoes, barbecue sauce, brown sugar, vinegar, chili powder, dried mustard, salt and cayenne pepper. Mix well. Transfer to freezer bags or a greased 2-quart casserole dish. Cover and freeze.

To prepare

Thaw in refrigerator or microwave. Preheat oven to 350°. Cover and bake for 60 to 70 minutes. Beans can be prepared in a slow cooker on low for 4 to 5 hours.

FREEZE
up to 6 months
(3 months if using frozen meat.)

15

Three Bean Casserole

1 lb. pork breakfast sausage
1 medium onion, chopped
2 stalks celery, chopped
2 tsp. minced garlic
1 (15 oz.) can kidney beans,
   drained
1 (15 oz.) can lima beans,
   drained

2 (15 oz.) cans white beans,
   drained
2 (8 oz.) cans tomato sauce
1 T. dried mustard
3 T. honey
1 1/2 T. vinegar
Dash of cayenne pepper
Salt and pepper to taste

In a medium skillet, brown sausage and drain off fat. Add onions, celery and garlic and continue to cook until tender. Remove from heat and combine with kidney beans, lima beans, white beans, tomato sauce, dried mustard, honey, vinegar, cayenne pepper, salt and pepper. Transfer to a greased 2 1/2-quart casserole dish or freezer bags. Cover and freeze.

To prepare

Preheat oven to 350°. Cover and bake frozen casserole for 60 to 70 minutes.

FREEZE
up to 6 months
(3 months if using frozen meat.)

Seafood &
Wild Rice Salad

1 T. olive oil
1 1/2 T. fresh lemon juice
1 tsp. curry powder
2/3 C. frozen peas
1/3 C. minced celery

4 T. chopped pimientos, optional
2 C. cooked wild rice
1/2 C. sour cream
2 (6 oz.) cans small shrimp,
  drained

In a medium bowl, mix together olive oil, lemon juice, curry powder, peas, celery, pimientos and cooked rice. Stir in sour cream and shrimp. Thoroughly blend. Freeze in a freezer bag or divided into serving-size portions.

To prepare

1 tomato, sliced
Torn salad greens

Chopped green onions

Thaw in refrigerator. Serve chilled with fresh sliced tomatoes, salad greens or green onions.

FREEZE
up to 2 months.

Tuna & Bean Salad

3 (15 oz.) cans Great Northern
    beans, well drained
4 T. diced pimientos
1 medium green pepper, diced
1 medium red onion, diced
3 T. dried parsley

1/4 C. olive oil
2 T. fresh lemon juice
1/2 tsp. salt
1/4 tsp. pepper
1 (6 oz.) can tuna, drained

In a mixing bowl, combine drained beans, pimientos, green peppers, red onions, parsley, olive oil, lemon juice, salt and pepper. Stir in drained tuna and thoroughly mix. Freeze in a freezer bag.

To prepare

Thaw in refrigerator. Serve chilled with fresh baby spinach or French bread.

FREEZE
up to 2 months.

Taco Salad

1 lb. lean ground beef	Dash of cayenne pepper
1 T. chili powder	1 (15 oz.) can kidney beans,
1 tsp. salt	drained
2 tsp. minced garlic	

In a skillet, brown beef and drain off fat. Add 1/3 cup water, chili powder, salt, garlic, cayenne pepper and drained kidney beans. Simmer for 10 minutes to allow flavors to combine. Freeze in freezer bags.

To prepare

Thaw in refrigerator. If using for a warm taco salad, cook gently over stovetop. Serve with tortilla chips or in taco salad shells on a bed of lettuce. Garnish with tomato wedges, black olives, shredded Cheddar cheese, green onions, avocado and sour cream.

FREEZE
up to 6 months
(3 months if using frozen meat.)

19

Rice & Spinach Salad

1 (10 oz.) pkg. frozen chopped
   spinach, thawed and
   drained
3 C. cooked wild rice
1 C. cooked white rice
1/4 C. sliced green onions
1/3 C. cooked and crumbled
   bacon

1/2 C. toasted sliced almonds*
1/3 C. vegetable oil
2 T. vinegar
2 T. soy sauce
1 1/2 T. honey

In a large mixing bowl, combine drained chopped spinach, cooked wild rice, cooked white rice, green onions, crumbled bacon and toasted almonds. In a separate bowl, whisk together vegetable oil, vinegar, soy sauce and honey. Toss together with rice mixture. Freeze in freezer bags.

* To toast, place almonds in a single layer on a baking sheet. Bake at 350° for approximately 10 minutes or until nuts are golden brown.

To prepare

Thaw in refrigerator. Serve chilled.

FREEZE
up to 6 months.

Tex-Mex Rice Salad

1 lb. ground beef	3 C. cooked rice
1/2 C. diced onion	1 (15 oz.) can garbanzo beans,
1/2 C. chili sauce	drained
1 T. minced garlic	1 (4 oz.) can chopped green
1/2 tsp. salt	chilies, drained
2 T. chili powder	

In a large skillet, brown beef and drain off fat. Add onions and continue to cook until tender. Allow to cool slightly. Add chili sauce, garlic, salt, chili powder, cooked rice, drained garbanzo beans and drained green chilies. Toss together. Freeze in freezer bags.

To prepare

1 C. shredded Cheddar cheese   2 medium tomatoes, diced

Thaw in refrigerator. Before serving, toss with shredded Cheddar cheese and diced tomatoes.

FREEZE
up to 6 months
(3 months if using frozen meat.)

Hearty Pork n' Beans

2 T. vegetable oil
1 1/2 lbs. chopped pork stew
   meat or pork cutlets
1 medium green pepper,
   chopped
1 medium onion, chopped
1 (16 oz.) can pork and beans
   with liquid

1 (15 oz.) can lima beans, drained
1 (15 oz.) can pinto beans,
   drained
1 C. ketchup
1/2 C. brown sugar
1 tsp. salt
1/2 tsp. garlic powder
1/4 tsp. pepper

In a large skillet, heat vegetable oil. Sauté pork over high heat until beginning to brown. Add green peppers and onions and cook until tender. In a soup or stock pot, combine sautéed meat, sautéed peppers and onions, pork and beans with liquid, drained lima beans, drained pinto beans, ketchup, brown sugar, salt, garlic powder and pepper. Thoroughly heat. Allow to cool slightly and transfer to a large freezer bag for freezing.

To prepare

Empty pork and beans into a slow cooker. Cook on low for 5 to 7 hours.

FREEZE
up to 6 months
(3 months if using frozen meat.)

22

Soups

Chili con Carne

Makes 2 - 2 1/2 quarts

1 1/2 lbs. lean ground beef
1 T. chopped garlic
1 medium onion, chopped
2 T. chili powder

1 (28 oz.) can tomatoes with juice
1 (15 oz.) can kidney beans,
    drained
3 beef bouillon cubes
1 (15 oz.) can tomato sauce

In a skillet, brown ground beef and drain off most of the fat. Add garlic and onions and sauté until tender. Add chili powder and stir over heat for 1 minute. Transfer to a large soup pot. Add tomatoes with juice, drained kidney beans, beef bouillon cubes and tomato sauce to soup pot and bring to a boil. Simmer for 15 minutes. Transfer to a freezer bag to freeze.

To prepare

Allow soup to thaw before heating on stovetop. Use a double boiler to heat frozen soup to avoid scorching the pan.

FREEZE
up to 6 months
(3 months if using frozen meat.)

Split Pea Soup

Makes 2 - 2 1/2 quarts

2 T. butter	**2 C. split green peas**
1 large carrot, diced	**1 bay leaf**
2 stalks celery, diced	**3/4 tsp. dried thyme**
1 medium onion, diced	
1 small to medium smoked ham hock	

In a medium soup pot, melt butter. Add diced carrots, celery and onions and sauté until softened, but not browned. Add ham hock, split peas, bay leaf, thyme and 8 cups water to soup pot. Bring to a boil then reduce to a simmer. Cook for 1 hour or until peas are tender. Be careful not to overcook before freezing, as soup will become too mushy when reheated. Transfer to a freezer bag to freeze.

To prepare

Allow soup to thaw before heating on stovetop. Use a double boiler to heat frozen soup to avoid scorching the pan.

FREEZE
up to 6 months.

25

Minestrone

Makes 2 1/2 quarts

1 T. olive oil
1 slice bacon, diced (optional)
2 T. chopped garlic
1 medium onion, chopped
2 stalks celery, chopped
1 large carrot, chopped
1 medium to large zucchini, chopped

3 chicken bouillon cubes
1 (15 oz.) can garbanzo or white beans, drained
1 (15 oz.) can diced tomatoes in juice
3/4 C. uncooked pasta (small pasta like Rotini or Orzo works best)

In a large soup pot, heat olive oil. If desired, add bacon and cook, draining off most of the fat. Add garlic, onions and celery to soup pot, sautéing until just limp. Add carrots, zucchini, chicken bouillon cubes, drained beans, tomatoes with juice and 8 cups water. Bring to a boil, then allow to simmer. Add uncooked pasta and simmer for 25 to 30 minutes. Transfer to a freezer bag to freeze.

To prepare

Allow soup to thaw before heating on stovetop. Use a double boiler to heat frozen soup to avoid scorching the pan.

FREEZE
up to 9 months.

French Onion Soup

Makes 2 quarts

3 T. butter	1/4 tsp. dried thyme
5 medium onions, thinly sliced	2 T. cooking sherry
1 T. brown sugar	3 beef bouillon cubes

In a medium soup pot, melt butter and add onions. Cook over medium heat, stirring occasionally until onions start to brown. Adjust to low heat, add brown sugar and continue cooking for 30 minutes, stirring occasionally. Onions should take on a slightly brown caramel color. Add thyme and sherry to soup pot and cook a few minutes until the alcohol evaporates. Add 3 3/4 cups water and beef bouillon cubes and bring to a boil, stirring until bouillon cubes are fully dissolved. Transfer to a freezer bag to freeze.

To prepare

Toasted French bread   **Shredded mozzarella cheese**

Allow soup to thaw before heating on stovetop. Use a double boiler to heat frozen soup to avoid scorching the pan. Ladle into ovenproof soup bowls and top with a slice of toasted French bread and grated mozzarella cheese. Broil or bake at 450° until cheese is melted and bubbling. If desired, toast and mozzarella cheese can be prepared separately in a broiler and placed on top of the soup without having to heat bowls in the oven.

FREEZE
up to 6 months.

27

Hearty Chicken Noodle Soup

Makes 1 1/2 to 2 quarts

1 T. butter	1/4 tsp. dried thyme
1 large carrot, chopped	3 chicken bouillon cubes
2 stalks celery, chopped	1 1/2 C. frozen egg noodles
1 bay leaf	1 1/2 C. diced chicken breast

In a medium soup pot, melt butter. Add carrots and celery. Sauté until cooked but not browned. Add 5 cups water, bay leaf, thyme and chicken bouillon cubes to soup pot. Bring to a boil and let simmer for about 10 minutes. Add egg noodles and simmer for an additional 20 minutes. Add diced chicken and return to a boil. Transfer to a freezer bag to freeze.

To prepare

Allow soup to thaw before heating on stovetop. Use a double boiler to heat frozen soup to avoid scorching the pan.

FREEZE

up to 6 months
(3 months if using frozen meat.)

Tortellini Soup

Makes 2 1/2 quarts

1 lb. ground or linked Italian sausage	1 large carrot, chopped
1 T. olive oil	3 chicken bouillon cubes
1 medium onion, chopped	1 bay leaf
2 T. chopped garlic	1/4 tsp. dried thyme
1 large yellow bell pepper, chopped	1 T. dried parsley
	2 C. small frozen cheese tortellini pasta

In a skillet, brown sausage and set aside to drain. If using ground Italian sausage, leave in small chunks that will hold their shape once added to the soup. If using links, allow to cool before slicing. In a medium soup pot, heat olive oil. Add onions, garlic and yellow peppers and sauté until limp but not browned. Add 6 cups water, carrots, chicken bouillon cubes, bay leaf, thyme and parsley and bring to a simmer. Add tortellini and browned Italian sausage and simmer until tortellini is just cooked. Transfer to a freezer bag to freeze.

To prepare

Allow soup to thaw before heating on stovetop. Use a double boiler to heat frozen soup to avoid scorching the pan.

FREEZE

up to 9 months
(6 months if using frozen meat.)

Wild Rice &
Chicken Stew

Makes 2 1/2 to 3 quarts

2 slices bacon, diced
1 T. vegetable oil
1 1/2 lbs. chicken breast
2 stalks celery, chopped
    with leaves
2 carrots, chopped
2 parsnips, chopped

1 large onion, chopped
2 T. chopped garlic
2 chicken bouillon cubes
1 bay leaf
1/2 C. uncooked wild rice
1 C. frozen sweet corn

In a medium soup pot, sauté diced bacon in vegetable oil until starting to brown. Add chicken breast and sear lightly. Remove chicken and bacon to a plate. Add celery, carrots, parsnips, onions, and garlic to the pot, sautéing until just limp. Add 9 cups water, chicken bouillon cubes, bay leaf and uncooked wild rice. Bring soup to a boil and add chicken. Simmer for 45 minutes or until rice and chicken are fully cooked. Turn off heat and remove chicken from pot. Allow chicken to cool before chopping it up. Return chicken and bacon to the stew and add corn. Transfer to a freezer bag to freeze.

To prepare

Allow soup to thaw before heating on stovetop. Use a double boiler to heat frozen soup to avoid scorching the pan.

FREEZE
up to 6 months
(3 months if using frozen meat.)

30

Creamy Butternut Squash Soup

Makes 1 1/2 quarts

1 large butternut squash	1/4 tsp. ginger
2 T. brown sugar	1 C. chicken broth, canned or
1/2 tsp. cinnamon	prepared with bouillon
1/4 tsp. nutmeg	

Preheat oven to 350°. Cut squash in half lengthwise and remove seeds. Bake in a casserole dish, face down, with 1/4" water for 45 minutes or until tender to the touch. Remove from oven and allow to cool. With a spoon, scoop meat from squash and place into a blender or food processor. Add brown sugar, cinnamon, nutmeg, ginger and chicken broth. Puree the mixture. Transfer to a freezer bag to freeze.

To prepare

1 pint half n' half	Sour cream
Chopped parsley	

Heat frozen soup over double boiler until warm. Stir in half n' half and continue to heat until piping hot and ready to serve. Serve with chopped parsley and a dollop of sour cream.

FREEZE
up to 9 months.

31

Double Corn Chowder

Makes 1 1/2 quarts

3 slices bacon, diced
1 onion, chopped
2 C. frozen corn
1 (14 oz.) can creamed corn

1 (14 oz.) can chicken broth
2 C. frozen hash brown potatoes,
thawed

In a large saucepan, cook diced bacon until crisp. Remove cooked bacon, drain on paper towels and crumble. Cook onions in bacon drippings in saucepan until just browned. Add bacon, frozen corn, creamed corn, chicken broth, 1 cup water and hash browns. Cover and bring to a boil. Reduce heat and let simmer for 10 to 15 minutes. Transfer to a freezer bag to freeze.

To prepare

3/4 C. milk, whole or 2%

Heat frozen soup in a double boiler or over low heat, stirring often. Add whole or 2% milk. Stir and serve.

FREEZE
up to 6 months.

Beef Barley Vegetable Soup

Makes 2 1/2 to 3 quarts

2 T. vegetable oil
1 1/2 lbs. beef stew meat, cubed
1 large onion, chopped
1 bell pepper, chopped
1 tsp. dried thyme
1 bay leaf

4 beef bouillon cubes
1 (28 oz.) can diced tomatoes
  in juice
2/3 C. uncooked barley
1 C. frozen green beans
1 C. frozen corn

In a medium soup pot, heat vegetable oil. Brown the beef stew meat over high heat and remove with a slotted spoon. Over medium heat, sauté onions and bell peppers in soup pot until just tender. Return meat to soup pot. Add 3 1/2 cups water, thyme, bay leaf and beef bouillon cubes and simmer for 45 minutes to 1 hour. Add tomatoes with juice, barley, green beans and corn and simmer for an additional 25 minutes. Transfer to a freezer bag to freeze.

To prepare

Allow soup to thaw before heating on stovetop. Use a double boiler to heat frozen soup to avoid scorching the pan.

FREEZE
up to 6 months
(3 months if using frozen meat.)

Farmhouse Chili

Makes 2 to 2 1/2 quarts

1 lb. pork sausage	1 T. maple syrup
1 large onion, chopped	2 tsp. ground cumin
2 stalks celery, chopped	1 tsp. dried sage
1 (28 oz) can whole tomatoes	1/2 tsp. pepper
in juice, coarsely chopped	2 (15 oz.) cans Great Northern or
2 C. chicken broth, canned or	other white beans, drained
prepared with bouillon	

In a large soup pot, brown pork sausage and drain off fat. Add onions and celery and sauté, with drained sausage, until just tender. Add chopped tomatoes with juice, chicken broth, maple syrup, ground cumin, sage, pepper and drained beans to soup pot. Bring to a boil. Reduce heat and let simmer for about 20 minutes. Transfer to a freezer bag to freeze.

To prepare

Allow soup to thaw before heating on stovetop. Use a double boiler to heat frozen soup to avoid scorching the pan.

FREEZE
up to 6 months
(3 months if using frozen meat.)

Black Bean Stew

2 T. olive oil
1 large onion, chopped
4 stalks celery, chopped
2 T. minced garlic
2 carrots, chopped

1 ham hock
1 lb. black beans, rinsed and
   soaked
3 chicken bouillon cubes

In a medium soup pot, heat olive oil. Add onions, celery, garlic and carrots and sauté. Add ham hock, drained beans, chicken bouillon cubes and 10 cups water. Bring to a boil. Reduce heat and let simmer for approximately 2 hours, until beans are tender. Transfer to a freezer bag to freeze.

To prepare

Heat frozen soup gently over stovetop. Simmer for 15 minutes or until soup reaches desired thickness. If desired, serve with sour cream and Cheddar cheese.

FREEZE
up to 6 months.

Beef Stew

Makes 1 1/2 to 2 quarts

1 T. vegetable oil	1/2 tsp. dried thyme
1 lb. beef stew meat, cubed	Salt and pepper to taste
2 stalks celery, chopped	2 medium carrots, chopped
1 medium onion, chopped	1 large potato, chopped
1 beef bouillon cube	1 medium turnip, chopped
1 bay leaf	

In a medium soup pot, heat vegetable oil and brown the beef stew meat. Add celery and onions and cook until just tender. Add beef bouillon cube, bay leaf, thyme and 4 cups water. Bring to a boil. Reduce heat and let simmer for 1 hour. Add salt and pepper, if desired. Add carrots, potatoes and turnips. Simmer for about 1 additional hour. Transfer to a freezer bag to freeze.

To prepare

3 T. flour

Heat frozen soup gently over stovetop. In a small bowl, whisk together flour and 1/2 cup cold water and add to stew. Simmer for 15 minutes or until soup reaches desired thickness.

FREEZE
up to 6 months
(3 months if using frozen meat.)

Irish Stew

Makes 2 1/2 quarts

2 medium onions, sliced	2 tsp. salt
1 T. butter	1/2 tsp. pepper
2 lbs. lamb stew meat, cubed, trimmed of fat	
2 lbs. (about 6 medium) red or gold potatoes, chopped to bite-size pieces	

In a medium to large soup pot, lightly brown onions in butter. Layer lamb stew meat and potatoes in pot and sprinkle with salt and pepper. Cover with water to 1" over top of potatoes and cubed lamb meat. Bring to a boil and simmer for about 1 hour, until lamb and potatoes are cooked, but not overly tender. Transfer to a freezer bag to freeze.

To prepare

1/2 to 1 1/2 C. dark beer

Gently warm frozen soup to boiling over stovetop and add dark beer to taste.

FREEZE
up to 6 months
(3 months if using frozen meat.)

Brunswick Stew

3 slices bacon, diced
2 lbs. chicken breast, cubed
1 medium onion, chopped
1 (28 oz.) can whole tomatoes
    with juice, coarsely chopped
1 (15 oz.) can whole kernel corn
    with juice

1 (15 oz.) can lima beans, drained
1 medium to large potato, cubed
1 chicken bouillon cube
1 bay leaf
3 T. flour

In a medium soup pot, brown bacon to cook off some of the fat. Add chicken and cook until chicken is browned. Add onions, chopped tomatoes with juice, corn with juice, drained lima beans, cubed potatoes, chicken bouillon cube and bay leaf. Bring to a boil and simmer for about 30 minutes, until potatoes are tender. In a small bowl, whisk together 1/2 cup water and flour. Stir flour mixture into soup and simmer for an additional 10 minutes as soup thickens. Remove from heat and allow to cool slightly before freezing. Transfer to a freezer bag to freeze.

To prepare

Heat frozen soup gently over stovetop. Simmer for 15 minutes or until soup reaches desired thickness.

FREEZE
up to 6 months
(3 months if using frozen meat.)

Manhattan Clam Chowder

3 slices bacon, diced
1 medium onion, diced
2 stalks celery, diced
2 medium potatoes, cubed
1/2 tsp. dried thyme
1 T. dried parsley

1 (15 oz.) can whole tomatoes
    with juice, coarsely chopped
2 (8 oz.) can chopped or whole
    baby clams with juice
Salt and pepper to taste

In a medium soup pot, brown diced bacon to cook off some of the fat. Add onions and celery, continuing to cook until vegetables are tender. Add 2 3/4 cups water, cubed potatoes, thyme, parsley and chopped tomatoes with juice. Bring to a boil and simmer for 30 minutes or until potatoes are tender. Stir in clams with juice and thoroughly heat. Season with salt and pepper before freezing. Transfer to a freezer bag to freeze.

To prepare

Heat frozen soup gently over stovetop. Simmer for 15 minutes or until soup reaches desired thickness.

FREEZE
up to 3 months.

Navy Bean Soup

1 lb. dried navy beans
1 T. vegetable oil
1 medium onion, chopped

1 smoked ham hock
1 1/2 C. smoked diced ham
1 bay leaf

Soak beans in water overnight. In a medium soup pot, heat vegetable oil. Sauté onions in vegetable oil until almost tender. Add ham hock, diced ham, 7 cups water, bay leaf and drained beans. Simmer for 1 1/2 to 2 hours, until beans are tender. Transfer to a freezer bag to freeze.

Variations

May substitute 3 cans navy beans for dried beans. Also, may substitute an additional cup of diced ham for the ham hock. Adjust the water, eliminating about 1/2 to 2/3 of the water so the soup is not too thin. Simmer for about 30 minutes before freezing.

To prepare

Heat frozen soup gently over stovetop. Simmer for 15 minutes or until soup reaches desired thickness.

FREEZE
up to 6 months
(3 months if using frozen meat.)

Gazpacho

1 1/2 C. tomato juice	1/4 C. minced red onion
1/2 C. cucumber, diced	2 tomatoes, chopped
1/2 C. green pepper, diced	

For aesthetic purposes, be careful to cut vegetables in small, semi-uniform pieces. In a large bowl, combine tomato juice, cucumber, green peppers, red onions and tomatoes. Transfer to a freezer bag to freeze.

To prepare

1/2 C. finely diced cucumber	1/4 C. chopped fresh parsley
1/2 C. finely diced yellow	2 T. fresh lemon juice
bell pepper	2 T. olive oil
3 stalks diced green onion	

Thaw in refrigerator. Transfer to a serving bowl and add finely diced cucumber, finely diced yellow bell pepper, diced green onions, chopped parsley, lemon juice and olive oil.

FREEZE
up to 1 month.

41

White Chili

1 T. vegetable oil
1 medium onion, chopped
1 T. minced garlic
1 stalk celery, diced
2 (15 oz.) cans Great Northern
    beans, drained

2 C. cooked cubed chicken
3 chicken bouillon cubes
1 (4 oz.) can chopped green
    chilies, drained

In a medium soup pot, heat vegetable oil. Add onions, garlic and celery and sauté until tender. Add drained beans, cooked chicken, 3 cups water, chicken bouillon cubes and drained green chilies. Bring to a boil. Simmer for 25 to 35 minutes. Allow to cool slightly before freezing. Transfer to a freezer bag to freeze.

To prepare

Heat frozen soup gently over stovetop. Simmer for 15 minutes or until soup reaches desired thickness.

FREEZE
up to 6 months
(3 months if using frozen meat.)

Curried Chicken and Rice Soup

1/2 C. butter	1/2 C. flour
2 medium carrots, diced	4 C. chicken broth, canned or
1 medium onion, diced	prepared with bouillon
2 stalks celery, diced	3 (12 oz.) cans evaporated milk
1 tsp. salt	2 1/2 C. cooked cubed chicken
1 1/2 tsp. curry powder	2 C. cooked rice

In a large soup pot, melt butter and sauté carrots, onions and celery until tender. Add salt and curry powder and sauté about 1 minute until curry is fragrant. Stir in flour to make a paste and pour in chicken broth. Bring to a boil and simmer for 15 minutes. Add evaporated milk, cooked chicken and cooked rice. Thoroughly heat before freezing. Transfer to a freezer bag to freeze.

To prepare

Thaw in refrigerator or microwave. Reheat gently in double boiler over medium heat, stirring constantly.

FREEZE
up to 3 months.

Tomato Corn Chowder

4 slices bacon, diced
1 large onion, chopped
1 (28 oz.) can diced tomatoes in
    juice
2 (15 oz.) cans whole kernel
    corn, drained

4 medium red potatoes, cut into
    1/2" cubes with skin
1 bay leaf

In a medium soup pot, sauté diced bacon and drain off fat, leaving roughly 1 to 1 1/2 tablespoons fat. Add onions to soup pot and sauté until tender. Add tomatoes with juice, drained corn, cubed potatoes and bay leaf. Bring to a boil and simmer for 30 minutes or until potatoes are just done.

To prepare

Thaw in refrigerator or microwave. Reheat on stovetop, stirring occasionally.

FREEZE
up to 6 months.

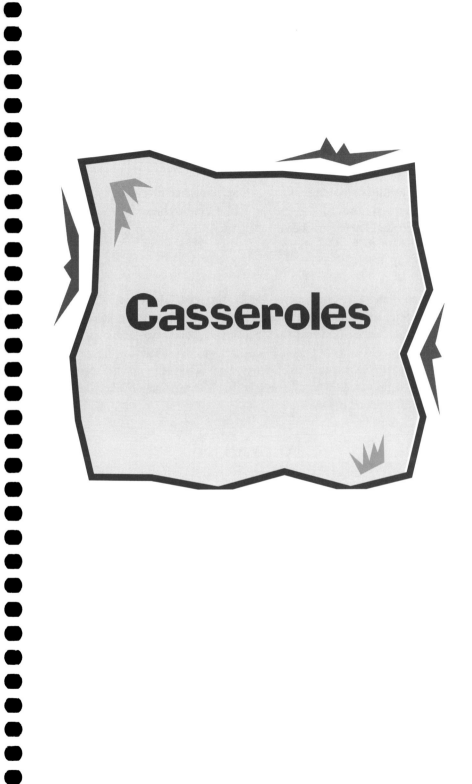

Casseroles

Macaroni &
Cheese with Ham

Makes 1 1/2 quarts

2 1/2 C. white sauce (page 10)
1/2 tsp. dried mustard
1/3 C. grated Parmesan cheese
2 C. shredded Cheddar cheese,
    divided

8 oz. uncooked macaroni
1 1/2 C. cubed ham

Prepare white sauce or reheat previously frozen white sauce using a double boiler. Stir in dried mustard, Parmesan cheese and 1 1/2 cups Cheddar cheese, stirring until cheese is melted. Cook macaroni in boiling water until just done, cool under cold water and drain. Place macaroni and cubed ham in a greased 2-quart casserole dish and toss together. Pour white sauce mixture over all, stirring slightly to allow sauce to seep in. Top with remaining 1/2 cup Cheddar cheese. Cover and freeze.

To prepare

Preheat oven to 375°. Cover frozen casserole and bake for 25 minutes. Uncover and bake for an additional 25 minutes, until hot and bubbly.

FREEZE
up to 9 months
(6 months if using frozen meat.)

46

Chicken Stew
& Biscuits

Makes 2 quarts

1 T. vegetable oil	1 1/2 C. sliced mushrooms
1 small to medium onion,	1 1/2 C. frozen peas
chopped	3 C. chicken broth, canned or
4 stalks celery, chopped	prepared with bouillon
1 T. chopped garlic	3 T. cornstarch
3 medium carrots, chopped	3 C. diced chicken

In a medium soup pot, add oil and heat. Add onions, celery and garlic and sauté until just tender. Add carrots, mushrooms, peas and chicken broth. Bring to a boil and simmer for 10 minutes. In a small bowl, whisk cornstarch and 1/3 cup cold water together. Stir cornstarch mixture into simmering stew as it thickens to the consistency of gravy. Stir in diced chicken. Pour all into a greased 2-quart casserole dish. Cover and freeze.

To prepare

1 tube of 10 biscuits

Preheat oven to 375°. Thaw casserole in microwave. Cover and bake in oven for 25 minutes. Uncover and arrange biscuits over the top, allowing them to overlap if space requires. Bake casserole for an additional 25 minutes, until biscuits are golden brown and stew is bubbling.

FREEZE
up to 9 months
(6 months if using frozen meat.)

Cannelloni with Cheese Sauce

Makes 4 to 6 servings

1/4 lb. ground beef	1 C. white sauce (page 10)
1/4 lb. Italian sausage	1 C. shredded mozzarella
1/2 C. chopped onion	cheese, divided
2 C. marinara sauce (page 9)	1/4 C. grated Parmesan cheese
6 large cannelloni pasta	

In a medium skillet, brown beef and Italian sausage together and drain off fat. Add onions and cook until onions are just limp. Stir together with marinara sauce to make filling. Cook cannelloni pasta in boiling water until flexible but not fully cooked. Cool under cold water and drain. Fill cannelloni with meat and marinara mixture and pack firmly into a greased 2-quart baking dish. To make cheese sauce, warm white sauce and stir in 3/4 cup mozzarella cheese. Pour over stuffed cannelloni. In a small bowl, mix Parmesan cheese and remaining 1/4 cup mozzarella cheese and sprinkle over all. Cover and freeze.

To prepare

Preheat oven to 400°. Loosely cover and bake frozen casserole for 45 minutes. Remove cover and bake an additional 20 minutes, until cannelloni is hot and bubbly and cheese is slightly browned.

FREEZE

up to 6 months
(3 months if using frozen meat.)

48

Tuna Alfredo Casserole

2 1/2 C. uncooked pasta, such as bowtie, rigatoni or small penne	1 (12 oz.) can solid white tuna, drained
2/3 C. shredded mozzarella cheese	1 tsp. garlic powder
	1 tsp. dried basil
1/2 C. fresh grated Parmesan cheese	2 tsp. dried parsley
	1 1/2 C. white sauce (page 10)

Cook pasta in boiling water until just done, rinse under cold water and drain before transferring to a greased 2-quart casserole dish. Toss together the mozzarella and Parmesan cheese. Setting aside 1/3 cup of the cheese mix, toss the remainder with pasta in casserole dish. Combine drained tuna, garlic powder, basil, parsley and white sauce in a double boiler and heat all together. Pour over pasta mixture and stir to combine. Top with reserved 1/3 cup cheese mix. Cover and freeze.

To prepare

Preheat oven to 375°. Lightly cover and bake frozen casserole for 25 minutes. Uncover and cook for an additional 25 minutes, until casserole is hot and bubbly.

FREEZE
up to 3 months.

49

Chicken Tortellini Casserole

Makes 2 quarts

2 1/2 C. small frozen cheese
   tortellini pasta
1 1/2 C. frozen broccoli
2 C. cooked diced chicken,
   fresh or canned
1/2 C. grated Parmesan cheese
1 C. shredded mozzarella cheese

1 1/2 C. white sauce (page 10)
2 to 3 T. butter, melted
2/3 C. bread crumbs
1/2 tsp. dried basil
1 tsp. dried parsley
1/2 tsp. dried oregano

In a medium pot, cook tortellini according to package directions. Add broccoli for final minute of cooking time to allow it to thaw and warm. Drain and rinse in cold water. In a medium bowl, toss together tortellini, broccoli, cooked chicken, Parmesan and mozzarella cheese. Transfer to a greased 2-quart casserole dish. Pour white sauce over all and stir to combine. In a small bowl, combine melted butter, bread crumbs, basil, parsley and oregano. Sprinkle mixture over top of casserole. Cover and freeze.

To prepare

Preheat oven to 375°. Lightly cover and bake frozen casserole for 30 minutes. Remove cover and bake an additional 20 to 25 minutes.

FREEZE
up to 6 months.

Chicken Potato Casserole

Makes 2 quarts

1 (10 oz.) can cream of
    chicken soup
1 C. sour cream
1/4 C. milk
1 C. cooked diced chicken,
    fresh or canned
2 1/2 C. shredded Cheddar
    cheese, divided

3 1/2 C. frozen shredded
    hash browns, thawed
1 small onion, diced
1 medium bell pepper, diced
1 1/2 C. crushed potato chips

In a medium bowl, combine cream of chicken soup, sour cream, milk, cooked chicken, 1 3/4 cups Cheddar cheese, hash browns, onions and bell peppers. Mix all together and transfer to a greased 2-quart casserole dish. Top with remaining 3/4 cup Cheddar cheese and crushed potato chips. Cover and freeze.

To prepare

Preheat oven to 375°. Lightly cover and bake frozen casserole for 35 to 40 minutes. Uncover and bake an additional 25 to 30 minutes.

FREEZE
up to 6 months.

Crispy Chicken & Rice Casserole

3 1/2 C. cooked rice
2 C. cooked diced chicken
2 (10 oz.) cans cream of
  mushroom soup
1 (8 oz.) can sliced water
  chestnuts, drained
1 (4 oz.) can sliced mushrooms,
  drained

2 stalks celery, chopped
3/4 C. mayonnaise
1 small onion, chopped
1/2 C. sliced almonds
1 T. lemon juice
1 tsp. salt
3 T. butter, melted
1 C. crushed cornflakes

In a large mixing bowl, combine cooked rice, cooked chicken, cream of mushroom soup, drained water chestnuts, drained sliced mushrooms, celery, mayonnaise, onions, almonds, lemon juice and salt. Transfer to a greased 2-quart casserole dish. In a small bowl, combine melted butter and crushed cornflakes. Sprinkle mixture over top of casserole and freeze.

To prepare

Thaw overnight in refrigerator. Preheat oven to 350°. Cover and bake for 45 to 50 minutes. Uncover and bake for an additional 15 minutes.

FREEZE
up to 6 months
(3 months if using frozen meat.)

Eggplant Marinara Casserole

1/2 C. diced onions	1 large eggplant, peeled
2 T. minced garlic	and cut into 1/2" to
3 T. olive oil	1/4" slices, divided
2 C. grated ricotta cheese	1 tsp. dried thyme, divided
2 C. marinara sauce,	2 C. shredded mozzarella
divided (page 9)	cheese, divided

In a medium skillet, sauté onions and garlic in olive oil. Remove from heat and let cool. Add ricotta cheese, mix and set aside. Lightly grease a 2-quart casserole dish. Spoon 3 tablespoons marinara sauce in the casserole dish, making sure to completely cover the bottom. Layer half of each of the following: eggplant, marinara sauce, dried thyme, mozzarella cheese, and onion and ricotta mixture. Repeat layers. Cover and freeze.

To prepare

Preheat oven to 350°. Cover and bake frozen casserole for 45 minutes. Uncover and bake an additional 10 to 15 minutes.

FREEZE
up to 6 months.

53

Mexican Beef & Rice Casserole

1 lb. lean ground beef
1 medium red onion, diced
1 T. minced garlic
1 medium green pepper, diced

3 C. cooked rice
2 C. salsa, any kind
1/3 C. chopped black olives

In a large skillet, brown beef and drain off fat. Add onions, garlic and green peppers. Cook until vegetables are tender. Remove from heat. Toss together with cooked rice, salsa and olives. Transfer to a greased 2-quart casserole dish. Cover and freeze.

To prepare

Thaw in refrigerator or microwave. Preheat oven to 350°. Cover and bake for 45 to 50 minutes.

FREEZE
up to 6 months
(3 months if using frozen meat.)

Red Beans & Rice with Bacon

4 slices bacon, diced
1 medium onion, diced
1 (15 oz.) can red beans, drained
3/4 C. chicken broth, canned or prepared with bouillon

3 C. cooked rice
1 C. shredded Cheddar cheese, divided

In a medium skillet, sauté diced bacon until most of the fat is extracted, pouring off half. Add onions and continue to cook until tender. Add drained beans and chicken broth to skillet and bring to a boil. Simmer for about 10 minutes. Remove from heat and toss together with rice and 1/2 cup Cheddar cheese. Transfer to a greased 1 1/2-quart casserole dish. Top with remaining 1/2 cup Cheddar cheese. Cover and freeze.

To prepare

Thaw in refrigerator or microwave. Preheat oven to 350°. Cover and bake for 35 to 40 minutes. Remove cover and bake an additional 10 minutes.

FREEZE
up to 6 months.

Lasagna Roll-Ups

12 lasagna noodles
1 lb. ground beef or Italian
  sausage
1 medium red onion, diced
2 tsp. minced garlic
1 (8 oz.) can sliced mushrooms,
  drained
1 (15 oz.) jar spaghetti sauce
2 C. grated ricotta cheese

1 (10 oz.) pkg. frozen chopped
  spinach, thawed and
  well-drained
1/4 C. grated Parmesan cheese
1/3 C. shredded mozzarella
  cheese
1 tsp. dried basil
1/2 tsp. dried oregano
1 egg

Cook lasagna noodles according to package directions. Rinse and cool under cold water, drain and set aside. In a medium skillet, brown beef and drain off fat. Add onions and garlic, cooking until tender. Add mushrooms and spaghetti sauce and simmer for 10 minutes before removing from heat. In a medium bowl, combine ricotta cheese, spinach, Parmesan cheese, mozzarella cheese, basil, oregano and egg. Fill lasagna noodles, one at a time, with about 1/3 cup of the cheese and spinach mixture over half of the length of the noodle. Roll noodles up, beginning with the filled end. Pour 1 cup sauce mixture into the bottom of a greased 9x13" pan and spread evenly. Arrange roll-ups laying flat in the pan. Top with remaining sauce mixture. Cover and freeze.

To prepare

Thaw in refrigerator or microwave. Preheat oven to 350°. Cover and bake for 45 minutes. Remove cover and bake an additional 15 minutes.

FREEZE
up to 3 months.

Pork Fried Rice

2 T. vegetable oil	3 green onions, sliced
1 lb. pork loin, diced	1/2 C. diced red pepper
1 (4 oz.) can sliced mushrooms,	3/4 C. frozen peas
drained	3 C. cooked rice

In a large skillet, heat vegetable oil. Over high heat, sauté pork until browned and fully cooked. Add mushrooms, onions, red peppers and peas. Toss a few times to thoroughly heat. In a medium mixing bowl, combine pork and vegetable mixture with cooked rice. Stir together and transfer to a freezer bag to freeze.

To prepare

1 1/2 T. sesame oil	3 T. soy sauce
2 eggs	

Thaw in refrigerator or microwave. In a large sauté pan, heat sesame oil. Lightly beat eggs and set aside. Add pork fried rice to skillet and sauté over high heat, stirring constantly. Stir in soy sauce, continuing to cook over high heat. When heated through, make an open well in center of rice and pour in eggs. With a spoon, stir eggs as they fry, gradually incorporating them in with the fried rice.

FREEZE
up to 6 months.

Macaroni Casserole

1 1/2 C. dry macaroni, cooked
1 1/2 C. cooked diced chicken
   or turkey
1 C. shredded Cheddar cheese
1 C. milk
1/2 tsp. curry powder

1 (10 oz.) can cream of chicken
   soup
1 (4 oz.) can sliced mushrooms,
   drained
1/2 C. pimientos, drained
1 C. crushed potato chips

In a large pot, cook macaroni in boiling water. Drain and set aside. In a large mixing bowl, combine diced chicken, Cheddar cheese, milk, curry powder, cream of chicken soup, sliced mushrooms, pimientos and cooked macaroni. Mix well. Transfer to a greased 2-quart casserole dish. Top with crushed potato chips. Cover and freeze.

To prepare

Thaw in refrigerator or microwave. Preheat oven to 350°. Cover and bake for 35 to 45 minutes. Remove cover and bake an additional 10 to 15 minutes.

FREEZE
up to 3 months.

Turkey & Biscuit Pie

**2 C. cooked diced turkey
or chicken
1 C. frozen green beans
1 (10 oz.) can cream of
chicken soup**

**1 1/2 C. frozen corn
1/2 C. chicken broth, canned
or prepared with bouillon**

In a large mixing bowl, combine diced turkey, green beans, cream of chicken soup, corn and chicken broth. Transfer to a greased 2-quart casserole dish. Cover and freeze.

To prepare

1 tube buttermilk biscuits

Thaw in a refrigerator or microwave. Preheat oven to 375°. Arrange buttermilk biscuits across the top of the casserole. Slightly overlap biscuits if necessary. Bake for 30 to 40 minutes.

FREEZE
up to 3 months.

Beef & Hash Brown Casserole

4 C. frozen shredded hash browns	2 C. frozen green beans or other vegetable of choice
3 T. vegetable oil	1 (2.8 oz.) can French fried onions, divided
1 lb. ground beef	
1 small env. brown gravy mix	1 C. shredded Cheddar cheese, divided

Preheat oven to 350°. In a medium mixing bowl, combine hash browns and oil. Press into a greased 8" square baking dish. Place in oven and bake until potatoes are thawed and set, about 15 minutes. In a medium saucepan, brown beef and drain off fat. Add 1 cup water and gravy mix and bring to a boil, cooking a few minutes to thicken. Remove from heat. Stir in green beans, half of the fried onions and 1/2 cup Cheddar cheese. Pour beef mixture over hash browns. Top with remaining fried onions and 1/2 cup Cheddar. Cover and freeze.

To prepare

Thaw in refrigerator or microwave. Preheat oven to 350°. Cover and bake for 35 minutes. Remove cover and bake an additional 15 minutes.

FREEZE
up to 6 months
(3 months if using frozen meat.)

Nacho Chicken Casserole

4 C. cooked cubed chicken
1 lb. American cheese,
    cubed
2 (10 oz.) cans cream of
    chicken soup
1 (10 oz.) can diced tomatoes
    with green chilies, drained

1 medium onion, chopped
1/2 tsp. garlic powder
1/4 tsp. pepper
1 (14 oz.) pkg. tortilla chips,
    divided

In a large mixing bowl, combine cooked chicken, American cheese cubes, cream of chicken soup, tomatoes with green chilies, chopped onions, garlic powder and pepper. Toss together to combine. Crush tortilla chips and stir chips into mixture, reserving 1 cup for topping. Transfer mixture to a greased 9x13" baking dish. Top with reserved crushed chips. Cover and freeze.

To prepare

Thaw in refrigerator or microwave. Preheat oven to 350°. Cover and bake for 30 minutes. Remove cover and bake an additional 15 minutes.

Cheesy Beef n' Pasta

2 C. uncooked spiral or
   corkscrew pasta
2 lb. ground beef
1 large red onion, chopped
1 T. minced garlic
1 (4 oz.) can sliced mushrooms,
   drained

1 (26 oz.) jar spaghetti sauce or
   3 C. marinara sauce
   (page 9)
1 C. shredded Cheddar cheese
1/2 C. grated Parmesan cheese
2 C. shredded mozzarella cheese
1/2 C. sour cream

Cook pasta in boiling water until almost done. Cool under cold water, drain and set aside. In a medium saucepan, brown beef and drain off fat. Add onions and garlic. Sauté a few minutes longer until onions are tender but not browned. Add mushrooms and spaghetti sauce. Bring to a boil and simmer for 10 minutes. In a medium mixing bowl, combine Cheddar, Parmesan and mozzarella cheeses. Set aside. In a greased 2 1/2-quart casserole dish, evenly spread 1/2 cup of the meat sauce across the bottom. Put in half the pasta, then half of the remaining meat sauce. Add dollops of sour cream and 1/3 of the cheese mixture. Layer next with remaining pasta and meat sauce. Top with remaining cheese mixture.

To prepare

Thaw in refrigerator or microwave. Preheat oven to 350°. Cover and bake for 40 to 45 minutes. Remove cover and bake an additional 10 to 15 minutes.

FREEZE
up to 3 months.

Enchilada Casserole

1 1/2 lbs. ground beef	2 C. salsa, any kind, divided
1 large onion, chopped	8 (7") flour tortillas, divided
3 T. chili powder	3 C. frozen corn, divided
1 tsp. salt	1 C. sour cream, divided
1/2 tsp. pepper	4 C. shredded mozzarella
1/4 tsp. garlic powder	cheese, divided

In a medium sauté pan, brown beef and drain off fat. Add onions, cooking a few minutes more until onions are tender. Add 1 cup water, chili powder, salt, pepper and garlic powder. Bring to a boil and simmer for 10 minutes. Into the bottom of a greased 9x13" casserole dish, pour 1/2 cup salsa and spread evenly. Arrange 4 tortillas over the salsa. Top with half of the meat mixture. Add half of the remaining salsa, half of the corn, half of the sour cream and half of the mozzarella cheese. Cover with remaining 4 tortillas. Add remaining meat mixture, salsa, corn, sour cream and mozzarella cheese. Cover and freeze.

To prepare

Thaw in refrigerator or microwave. Preheat oven to 350°. Cover and bake for 35 minutes. Remove cover and bake an additional 10 to 15 minutes.

FREEZE
up to 3 months.

Green Bean Chicken Casserole

1 pkg. Uncle Ben's long
   grain and wild rice mix
4 C. cooked cubed chicken
2 C. frozen French-cut
   green beans
1 (10 oz.) can cream of
   mushroom soup

1 (10 oz.) can cream of
   chicken soup
1 (4 oz.) can sliced mushrooms,
   drained
1 small onion, chopped
1 C. shredded Cheddar cheese

Cook rice according to package directions. Set aside to cool slightly. In a large mixing bowl, combine cooked rice, cubed chicken, green beans, cream of mushroom soup, cream of chicken soup, drained mushrooms, onions and Cheddar cheese. Place in a greased 2 1/2-quart baking dish. Cover and freeze.

To prepare

Fried onions for topping, optional

Thaw in refrigerator or microwave. Preheat oven to 350°. Cover and bake for 45 to 50 minutes. Remove cover and bake an additional 10 to 15 minutes. If desired, top with fried onions.

FREEZE
up to 3 months.

Tex-Mex Macaroni Casserole

1 (7 oz.) pkg. uncooked macaroni	1 (6 oz.) can tomato paste
2 lbs. ground beef	1 (4 oz.) can chopped green
1 large onion, chopped	chilies, drained
1 T. minced garlic	1 tsp. salt
1 (28 oz.) can diced tomatoes	1 T. chili powder
in juice	1/2 tsp. ground cumin
1 (16 oz.) can kidney beans,	2 C. shredded Monterey
drained	Jack cheese

Cook macaroni in boiling water until almost done. Cool under cold water, drain and set aside. In a large saucepan, brown beef and drain off fat. Add onions and garlic. Sauté a few minutes more until onions are tender. Add tomatoes with juice, drained kidney beans, tomato paste, drained green chilies, salt, chili powder and ground cumin. Bring to a boil and simmer for 10 to 15 minutes. Stir in cooked macaroni. Transfer to a greased 2 1/2-quart baking dish or two smaller casserole dishes. Top with Monterey Jack cheese. Cover and freeze.

To prepare

Thaw in refrigerator or microwave. Preheat oven to 375°. Cover and bake for 35 minutes. Remove cover and bake an additional 10 minutes.

FREEZE
up to 6 months
(3 months if using frozen meat.)

Pineapple Ham & Rice

2 C. cooked rice
2 C. cubed ham
1 (20 oz.) can crushed
    pineapple, drained

1/2 C. brown sugar
1 tsp. lemon juice
1 tsp. ground mustard

In a medium mixing bowl, combine cooked rice, cubed ham, drained pineapple, brown sugar, lemon juice and ground mustard. Spoon mixture into a greased 1 1/2-quart baking dish. Cover and freeze.

To prepare

Thaw in refrigerator or microwave. Preheat oven to 350°. Cover and bake for 40 to 45 minutes.

FREEZE
up to 6 months
(3 months if using frozen meat.)

Chicken and Broccoli Bake

3 C. cooked cubed chicken
2 (10 oz.) cans cream of
    chicken soup
1 (10 oz.) pkg. frozen
    broccoli florets

1/4 C. milk
2 C. shredded Cheddar
    cheese, divided

Place cooked chicken in the bottom of a greased 2 1/2-quart baking dish. In a medium bowl, combine cream of chicken soup, broccoli, milk and 3/4 cup Cheddar cheese. Pour mixture over chicken in baking dish and top with remaining 1 1/4 cups Cheddar cheese.

To prepare

Thaw in refrigerator or microwave. Preheat oven to 375°. Cover and bake for 35 minutes. Remove cover and bake an additional 10 to 15 minutes.

FREEZE
up to 3 months.

Spanish Beef n' Noodles

1 lb. ground beef
4 slices bacon, diced
1 medium red onion, diced
1 medium green pepper,
   chopped
1 medium yellow pepper,
   chopped

1 (14 oz.) can diced tomatoes
   in juice
1/4 C. chili sauce
1 tsp. salt
3 C. medium egg noodles

In a medium saucepan, brown beef and diced bacon and drain off fat. Add onions, green peppers and yellow peppers. Sauté until vegetables are tender. Add tomatoes with juice, 1 cup water, chili sauce and salt. Bring to a boil. Reduce heat and let simmer for 10 minutes. Meanwhile, cook noodles according to package directions until almost done. Cool under cold water and drain. Add to beef mixture and pour all into a greased 2 1/2-quart casserole dish.

To prepare

Thaw in refrigerator or microwave. Preheat oven to 375°. Cover and bake for 45 minutes.

FREEZE
up to 6 months
(3 months if using frozen meat.)

Mexican Chicken Casserole

1 (10 oz.) can cream of chicken soup	1 medium onion, chopped
1 (10 oz.) can Cheddar cheese soup	1 pkg. flour or corn tortillas, divided
1 (10 oz.) can tomatoes with green chilies, drained	2 C. cooked coarsely chopped chicken, divided
1 1/4 C. milk, whole or 2%	1 1/2 C. shredded Cheddar cheese, divided

In a medium mixing bowl, combine cream of chicken soup, Cheddar cheese soup, tomatoes with green chilies, milk and onions and set aside. Tear tortillas into 1" wide strips. In a greased 2-quart casserole dish, make bottom layer using half of tortillas, chicken meat and 1 cup of Cheddar cheese. Cover with half of the soup mixture. Repeat for a second layer, pouring remaining soup mixture over the top and finishing with remaining 1/2 cup Cheddar cheese. Cover and freeze.

To prepare

Thaw in refrigerator or microwave. Preheat oven to 350°. Bake for 45 to 55 minutes, until hot and bubbly.

FREEZE
up to 3 months.

Southwestern Chicken & Rice Casserole

2 C. cooked rice
2 C. shredded Monterey
  Jack cheese, divided
1 1/2 C. cooked coarsely
  chopped chicken
1 C. evaporated milk

1/2 C. diced red onion
2 large eggs, lightly beaten
1/4 C. finely chopped cilantro
2 T. butter, melted
1 T. diced jalapenos
1/2 tsp. salt

In a medium mixing bowl, combine cooked rice, 1 1/2 cups Monterey Jack cheese, cooked chicken, evaporated milk, onions, eggs, cilantro, melted butter, jalapenos and salt. Transfer to a lightly greased 2-quart casserole dish and top with remaining 1/2 cup Monterey Jack cheese. Cover and freeze.

To prepare

Thaw overnight in refrigerator. Preheat oven to 350°. Cover and bake for 60 to 70 minutes. Remove covering for final 15 minutes of baking time.

FREEZE
up to 3 months.

Beef & Noodle Casserole

2 lbs. ground beef	1/2 C. sour cream
1/2 C. diced onions	1 1/2 C. cottage cheese
1/4 C. diced green peppers	1 (8 oz.) pkg. egg noodles,
2 (8 oz.) cans tomato sauce	divided
8 oz. cream cheese, softened	1 C. shredded Swiss cheese

In a medium sauté pan, brown beef. Drain off fat. Add onions and peppers and continue to sauté until just tender. Stir in tomato sauce and set aside. In a medium bowl, mix cream cheese, sour cream and cottage cheese. Set aside. Cook egg noodles in boiling water until slightly undercooked. Drain and rinse in cold water. In a lightly greased 2-quart casserole dish, layer half the noodles, half the cheese mixture and half the meat mixture. Repeat layers. Top with Swiss cheese. Cover and freeze.

To prepare

Thaw overnight in refrigerator. Preheat oven to 375°. Cover and bake for 45 to 50 minutes. Remove covering for final 10 to 15 minutes of baking time.

FREEZE
up to 3 months.

71

Ham & Rice with Broccoli Casserole

1 (10 oz.) can Cheddar cheese
    soup
1 (10 oz.) pkg. frozen broccoli
    florets
1 C. cooked rice

1 C. cubed ham
1/4 C. sour cream
1/3 C. milk
1 T. butter, melted
1/4 C. bread crumbs

In a medium mixing bowl, combine Cheddar cheese soup, broccoli, cooked rice, ham, sour cream and milk. In a separate bowl, toss melted butter with bread crumbs for topping. Transfer ham and rice mixture to a greased 1 1/2-quart casserole dish. Sprinkle bread crumb mixture over top. Cover and freeze.

To prepare

Thaw in refrigerator or microwave. Preheat oven to 350°. Cover and bake for 30 minutes. Remove cover and bake an additional 10 to 15 minutes.

FREEZE
up to 3 months.

72

Main Dishes

Marinated
Pork Loin Chops

1 lb. fresh boneless pork loin chops	3 T. olive oil
1 T. white wine vinegar	1 T. finely chopped garlic
1 1/2 T. fresh lemon juice	1 T. dried parsley flakes
1 T. Worcestershire sauce	1 tsp. dried thyme
	Salt & pepper to taste

Place pork loin chops in freezer bag. In a medium bowl, combine white wine vinegar, lemon juice, Worcestershire sauce, olive oil, garlic, parsley, thyme, salt & pepper. Pour over meat and freeze.

To prepare

Thaw meat in marinade mixture. Grill over barbecue or under oven broiler until well cooked. If desired, serve with a honey mustard dipping sauce, made by combining 6 tablespoons honey with 1/4 cup Dijon mustard.

FREEZE
up to 6 months.

Roast Chicken in Wine Sauce

4 chicken leg quarters
Salt & pepper
4 T. olive oil, divided
1 medium onion, chopped
1 T. chopped garlic
2 medium carrots, chopped

2 stalks celery, chopped
1 tsp. dried thyme
1/4 C. flour
3/4 C. dry white wine
1 1/4 C. chicken broth, canned
　　or prepared with bouillon

Pull skin from chicken leg quarters and sprinkle chicken lightly with salt and pepper. In a sauté pan, heat 2 tablespoons olive oil. Brown chicken pieces on all sides and remove to a greased 2-quart casserole dish. In the same pan, sauté onions, garlic, carrots, celery and thyme until just tender. Remove with a slotted spoon to casserole dish. Add remaining 2 tablespoons olive oil to sauté pan. Add flour to sauté pan and stir to combine, forming a paste. Add wine to hot pan and stir to combine with flour, allowing some of the alcohol to burn off. Add chicken broth and heat to boiling. Pour mixture over chicken and vegetables in casserole dish. Cover and freeze.

To prepare

Thaw in refrigerator or microwave. Preheat oven to 375°. Cover and bake approximately 1 1/2 hours, until chicken is fully cooked.

FREEZE
up to 6 months
(3 months if using frozen meat.)

Meatloaf with Rice Stuffing

1 lb. ground beef
3/4 C. bread crumbs
1 (8 oz.) can tomato sauce
1 medium onion, finely chopped
1 stalk celery, finely chopped
1 egg
1/4 tsp. dried marjoram

1/4 tsp. dried thyme
1 (4 oz.) can sliced mushrooms, drained
3/4 C. shredded Swiss cheese
1/2 C. cooked rice
1/2 lb. ground Italian sausage

In a large bowl, combine ground beef, bread crumbs, tomato sauce, onions, celery, egg, marjoram and thyme. Mix well. Pat into a microwavable bundt pan, pressing meat against sides and center tube of pan. Layer mushrooms, Swiss cheese, cooked rice and Italian sausage in the center of the meatloaf. Press edges of meat mixture over filling, sealing to cover completely. Cover bundt pan and freeze.

To prepare

Preheat oven to 350°. Thaw meatloaf in microwave. Cover and bake for 55 minutes. Remove cover and bake an additional 10 to 15 minutes.

FREEZE
up to 6 months
(3 months if using frozen meat.)

Beef & Cheese Burritos

Makes 10 burritos

1 lb. lean ground beef	1 3/4 C. shredded Monterey Jack
1 (1 1/4 oz.) pkg. taco seasoning	cheese, divided
3/4 C. grated ricotta cheese	2 1/2 C. salsa, any kind, divided
1 (7 oz.) can diced green chilies,	10 (8") flour tortillas
drained	

In a medium sauté pan, brown beef. Drain off fat, add 3/4 cup water and taco seasoning and cook until thickened. In a medium bowl, combine ricotta cheese, drained green chilies and 1 cup Monterey Jack cheese. Spread 1 cup salsa over the bottom of a greased 2-quart casserole dish. Fill tortillas with beef mixture (roughly 2 tablespoons in each) and cheese mixture (roughly 1 tablespoon in each). Close each tortilla and place over salsa in baking dish. Top with remaining 1 1/2 cups salsa and 3/4 cup Monterey Jack cheese. Cover and freeze.

To prepare

Thaw overnight in refrigerator. Preheat oven to 350°. Cover and bake for 45 to 50 minutes. Uncover for final 15 minutes of baking to allow cheese to brown slightly.

FREEZE
up to 6 months
(3 months if using frozen meat.)

Sloppy Joes

1 lb. ground beef	2 T. yellow mustard
1 lb. ground pork	1 T. minced garlic
1 medium onion, diced	2 beef bouillon cubes
2 (8 oz.) cans tomato sauce	1/2 tsp. dried oregano

In a large sauté pan, brown beef and pork together. Drain off fat. Add onions and sauté until just starting to brown. Add tomato sauce, mustard, garlic, beef bouillon cubes and oregano. Bring mixture to a boil and simmer for 10 minutes, stirring occasionally. Freeze in freezer bags or air-tight containers.

To prepare

Thaw in refrigerator or microwave. Warm on stovetop, adding a touch more water for a thinner consistency and to avoid scorching. Serve on buns.

FREEZE
up to 9 months
(6 months if using frozen meat.)

Steak Fajitas

Makes 4 to 8 fajitas

Juice of 2 limes	1/2 to 1 tsp. red pepper flakes
Juice of 1 lemon	1/4 tsp. ground cumin, optional
2 T. minced garlic	1/4 tsp. ground coriander
3 green onions, minced	1 lb. fresh sirloin steak, cut into
3 T. fresh chopped cilantro	thin strips

In a medium bowl, combine lime juice, lemon juice, garlic, onions, cilantro, red pepper flakes, cumin and coriander, creating a marinade. Slice steak and combine with marinade in a freezer bag. Mix well to fully coat steak. Freeze.

To prepare

2 T. vegetable oil	1 yellow bell pepper, sliced thin
1 medium onion, sliced thin	4 to 8 (8") flour tortillas
1 red bell pepper, sliced thin	

Thaw steak in marinade overnight in refrigerator. In a large skillet, heat vegetable oil. Brown steak over high heat, adding onions, red peppers and yellow peppers halfway through the cooking. Serve piping hot with tortillas and toppings of your choice, such as sour cream, lettuce or salsa.

FREEZE
up to 6 months.

79

Teriyaki Chicken

1 T. fresh minced ginger or
    1 tsp. dried ginger
1 T. chopped garlic or
    1 tsp. dried garlic
1 C. soy sauce

1/4 C. brown sugar
1/4 C. dry white wine
1 1/2 lb. fresh chicken breasts,
    use whole or cut into
    strips for stir fry

In a freezer bag, mix 1/4 cup water, ginger, garlic, soy sauce, brown sugar and white wine. Transfer to a freezer bag. Put chicken in marinade and freeze.

Variations

Also may try this recipe with chicken wings or with legs and thighs for grilled Teriyaki chicken.

To prepare

Thaw chicken overnight in refrigerator. Cook chicken breast or sauté chicken strips.

FREEZE
up to 6 months.

Chicken Enchiladas

1 medium onion, chopped
1/2 C. chopped green pepper
2 T. butter
3 C. cooked cubed chicken
1 (4 oz.) can chopped green
   chilies, drained
1 (10 3/4 oz) can cream of
   chicken soup

1 C. sour cream
1 C. shredded Monterey Jack
   cheese, divided
1 C. shredded Cheddar cheese,
   divided
1 C. enchilada sauce
12 (6") flour or corn tortillas

In a medium skillet, sauté onions and green peppers in butter. Add cooked chicken, remove from heat and set aside. In a medium mixing bowl, whisk together drained green chilies, cream of chicken soup and sour cream. Add chicken mixture, 1/2 cup Monterey Jack cheese and 1/2 cup Cheddar cheese. Stir together to form filling. Fill each tortilla with filling and place, seam side down, in a greased 2-quart casserole dish. Top with enchilada sauce and remaining 1/2 cup Monterey Jack and 1/2 cup Cheddar cheese.

To prepare

Thaw completely in refrigerator or microwave. Preheat oven to 350°. Bake, uncovered, for 35 to 45 minutes.

FREEZE
up to 6 months
(3 months if using frozen meat.)

81

Chicken Pot Pie

1 medium onion, chopped	2 1/4 C. chicken broth, canned or
2 carrots, chopped	prepared with bouillon
2 stalks celery, chopped	1 C. milk, whole or 2%
6 T. butter, divided	1 C. frozen peas
1/2 C. flour	3 C. cooked cubed chicken

In a medium skillet, sauté onions, carrots and celery in 2 tablespoons butter until softened but not browned. Set aside. In a medium saucepan, melt remaining 4 tablespoons butter over high heat, allowing it to bubble but not brown. With a whisk, stir in flour. Cook, stirring constantly, for about 1 minute. Gradually whisk in chicken broth, then milk. Bring mixture to a boil and simmer a few minutes to allow thickening. Stir in sautéed vegetables, peas and cooked chicken and remove from heat. Pour mixture into a greased 2-quart casserole dish. Cover and freeze.

To prepare

1 basic pie crust (page 106)

Thaw in refrigerator or microwave. Roll out pie crust and place over chicken stew mixture, tucking in edges of pie crust around the sides of the pan. Cut slits in top of crust to allow steam to vent out. Preheat oven to 375°. Bake, uncovered, for 35 to 45 minutes.

FREEZE
up to 6 months
(3 months if using frozen meat.)

82

Savory Meat Loaf

1 1/2 lbs. ground beef	1/2 C. ketchup
1 pkg. Lipton onion soup mix	1/4 C. bread crumbs
1 egg, lightly beaten	

In a medium mixing bowl, combine ground beef, soup mix, egg, ketchup and bread crumbs. Shape into a loaf. Line a loaf pan with foil first and then a layer of plastic wrap. Make sure that both pieces will be large enough to completely cover the meatloaf. Place meatloaf in loaf pan and seal the 2 wraps around the loaf. Place meatloaf in freezer for a couple hours. Once meatloaf is semi-frozen, remove it from loaf pan leaving foil and plastic around loaf. Place meatloaf back in freezer.

To prepare

Unwrap meatloaf, place in loaf pan and thaw in microwave or refrigerator overnight. Preheat oven to 350°. Bake, uncovered, for 65 to 75 minutes.

FREEZE
up to 6 months
(3 months if using frozen meat.)

Honey Glazed Pork Chops

1/2 C. honey
1/4 C. cider vinegar
1/2 tsp. ground ginger or
    1 T. fresh minced ginger

2 tsp. minced garlic
3 T. soy sauce
6 fresh boneless pork chops

In a small bowl, mix together honey, cider vinegar, ginger, garlic and soy sauce. Combine with pork chops in a plastic freezer bag. Freeze.

To prepare

Thaw meat in marinade mixture overnight in refrigerator. Arrange pork chops with marinade in baking dish. Preheat oven to 350°. Bake for 45 to 55 minutes. Turn pork chops occasionally, 2 or 3 times, during baking to coat with glaze.

FREEZE
up to 6 months.

Ham Loaf
or Ham Balls

1 lb. ground ham	1/2 C. cracker crumbs
1/2 lb. ground pork	1/3 C. milk, whole or 2%
1 medium onion, diced	2 eggs
1 tart apple, peeled, cored	1 tsp. dried mustard
and diced	1/4 tsp. nutmeg

In a large mixing bowl, combine ham, pork, onions, apples, cracker crumbs, milk, eggs, dried mustard and nutmeg. Work ingredients together by hand until thoroughly blended. Shape mixture into a loaf or 1" balls. For a ham loaf, line a loaf pan with foil first and then a layer of plastic wrap. Make sure that both pieces will be large enough to completely cover the ham loaf. Place ham loaf in loaf pan and seal the 2 wraps around the loaf. Place ham loaf in freezer for a couple hours. Once ham loaf is semi-frozen, remove it from loaf pan. Place ham loaf back in freezer, wrapped in plastic and foil. For ham balls, freeze, covered with plastic and foil, on a baking sheet for a couple hours before transferring to a freezer bag.

To prepare

Thaw completely in refrigerator or microwave for loaf (not necessary to thaw ham balls). Preheat oven to 350°. Bake ham loaf, uncovered, in a loaf pan for 65 to 75 minutes. Bake ham balls, uncovered, on a baking sheet for 65 to 75 minutes.

FREEZE
up to 6 months
(3 months if using frozen meat.)

Stuffed Pork Chops

6 fresh bone-in pork chops,
   approximately 1" to
   1 1/2" thick
1 1/2 C. whole kernel corn
1 1/2 C. bread crumbs
2 tsp. dried parsley

1 tsp. dried sage
1/4 C. minced onion
1 C. diced apples
1 egg
3 T. milk
2 T. vegetable oil

Using a sharp paring knife, cut a pocket in each pork chop by inserting the knife in the loin and cutting towards the bone. Create an open cavity in each loin and make sure to leave a hole large enough for stuffing. In a medium bowl, combine corn, bread crumbs, dried parsley, dried sage, onions, apples, egg and milk to create stuffing. Stuff each chop with the corn stuffing. Brown chops in vegetable oil. Let pork chops cool and freeze tightly wrapped in plastic and foil or in freezer bags.

To prepare

Preheat oven to 350°. Place chops in a glass baking dish and thaw in microwave. Bake for 60 to 70 minutes.

FREEZE
up to 6 months.

Italian Meatballs

1 lb. ground beef	2 T. minced garlic
1 lb. ground pork	1 tsp. dried oregano
2 eggs	1/2 tsp. dried thyme
1/2 C. grated Parmesan or	1/4 tsp. dried crushed rosemary
Romano cheese	2 T. olive oil
2 T. dried parsley	1 C. unseasoned bread crumbs

In a medium mixing bowl, combine beef, pork, eggs, cheese, parsley, garlic, oregano, thyme, rosemary, olive oil and bread crumbs. Blend together thoroughly by hand. Form into balls. Place on a baking sheet and cover in plastic and foil to freeze. Freeze for a couple hours on baking sheet before transferring to a freezer bag.

To prepare

Preheat oven to 350°. Place frozen meatballs on a baking sheet and bake, uncovered, for 45 to 55 minutes.

FREEZE

up to 6 months
(3 months if using frozen meat.)

87

Beef Brisket or Barbecued Beef

4 to 5 lbs. fresh beef brisket,
   trimmed of fat
1 1/2 tsp. salt
1/2 medium onion, sliced thin
3/4 C. ketchup
1/3 C. red wine or cider vinegar

2 T. brown sugar
2 T. Worcestershire sauce
1 1/2 tsp. liquid smoke
1/2 tsp. pepper
1 bay leaf, crushed

Place beef brisket in a roaster. Sprinkle salt over beef brisket. In a medium mixing bowl, combine onions, ketchup, vinegar, brown sugar, Worcestershire sauce, liquid smoke, pepper and crushed bay leaf. Pour mixture over brisket. Cover and bake in a roaster at 325° for 3 to 4 hours. Serve as a roast and/or chop and partition into freezer bags. Freeze chopped brisket for quick barbecued beef sandwiches.

To prepare

1 C. beef broth, canned or prepared with bouillon

Thaw in refrigerator or microwave. Preheat oven to 350°. Cover and bake for 90 minutes, adding beef broth. For barbecued beef, chop thawed meat and cook in a saucepan over stovetop with barbecue sauce.

FREEZE
up to 6 months.

88

Mushroom Minute Steaks

1/4 C. plus 2 T. flour, divided	1 small onion, sliced
2 tsp. salt	1/2 lb. fresh sliced mushrooms
1/2 tsp. pepper	2/3 C. red wine
4 T. butter, divided	1 C. frozen pearl onions
6 (roughly 2 lbs.) fresh beef	3/4 C. beef broth, canned or
cube steaks	prepared with bouillon

In a small bowl, mix together 1/4 cup flour, salt and pepper. Dust the steaks with the flour mixture. In a large skillet, heat 3 tablespoons butter. Fry steaks in butter to medium doneness, roughly 8 to 10 minutes on each side. Remove steaks to a greased 9x13" baking dish. Add remaining 1 tablespoon butter to the skillet and sauté onions and mushrooms until tender. Add remaining 2 tablespoons flour to skillet to form a paste. Add red wine and boil vigorously for 2 to 3 minutes to allow alcohol to evaporate and sauce to thicken. Stir in pearl onions and beef broth and simmer for 5 to 10 minutes. Pour over steaks, cover and freeze.

To prepare

Thaw in refrigerator or microwave. Preheat oven to 350°. Cover and bake for 35 to 40 minutes. Remove cover and bake an additional 15 minutes.

FREEZE
up to 6 months.

Smothered Sirloin Steak

1/4 C. plus 2 T. flour, divided
1 tsp. salt
1/4 tsp. pepper
4 T. olive oil, divided
1 1/2 lbs. fresh top sirloin steaks
    or roast, cut into 4 oz.
    portions
1 C. dry red wine

1 T. chopped garlic
2/3 C. pitted black olives
3 medium carrots, sliced
1 large red onion, chopped
2 stalks celery, sliced
1 bay leaf
Fresh parsley

In a small bowl, combine 1/4 cup flour, salt and pepper. Use mixture to dust steaks. In a large skillet, heat 2 tablespoons olive oil and fry steaks for 8 to 10 minutes on each side. Remove steaks to a 9x13" casserole dish. Add remaining 2 tablespoons flour and 2 tablespoons olive oil to skillet to form a paste. Add red wine and boil for 2 to 3 minutes. Add 1/2 cup water and allow to simmer a few minutes. Top steaks with garlic, black olives, carrots, red onions, celery, bay leaf and fresh parsley. Pour red wine sauce over all. Cover and freeze.

To prepare

Thaw in refrigerator or microwave. Preheat oven to 350°. Cover and bake for 35 to 40 minutes. Remove cover and bake an additional 15 minutes.

FREEZE
up to 6 months.

Swiss Steak

4 T. butter, divided	1 large yellow onion, sliced
1/4 C. plus 2 T. flour, divided	1 large green pepper, sliced
1/2 tsp. salt	1 (16 oz.) can whole tomatoes,
1 tsp. dried mustard	drained and coarsely
1 1/2 lbs. fresh top sirloin or	chopped
tenderized round steak,	2/3 C. beef broth, canned or
cut into 4 oz. portions	prepared with bouillon

In a large skillet, heat 3 tablespoons butter. In a medium bowl, combine 1/4 cup flour, salt and dried mustard. Use mixture to dust steaks. Fry steaks in butter to medium doneness, roughly 8 to 10 minutes on each side. Remove steaks to a greased 9x13" baking dish. Add remaining 1 tablespoon butter to skillet and sauté onions and peppers until tender. Add remaining 2 tablespoons flour to form a paste. Add drained tomatoes and beef broth and bring to a boil, allowing sauce to thicken. Simmer for about 10 minutes. Pour over steaks. Cover and freeze.

To prepare

Thaw in refrigerator or microwave. Preheat oven to 350°. Cover and bake for 35 to 40 minutes. Remove cover and bake an additional 15 minutes.

FREEZE
up to 6 months.

91

Stuffed Baked Potatoes

4 medium baking potatoes
1 T. butter, softened
1 lb. ground beef or pork
1 (14 oz.) can chopped tomatoes
    with cilantro, drained

1 (1 1/4 oz.) env. taco seasoning
1/3 C. shredded Cheddar cheese

Preheat oven to 375°. Brush potatoes with butter. Prick the potatoes with a fork and bake for 1 hour or until done. In a skillet, brown beef and drain off fat. Add drained tomatoes, taco seasoning and Cheddar cheese and set aside. Allow baked potatoes to cool before cutting in half. Use a spoon to scoop out the inside flesh, leaving about 1/2" layer of potato on the skin. Fill each potato with an equal amount of the beef and tomato filling. Wrap individually or place side by side in a baking dish to freeze. Cover and freeze.

To prepare

Thaw in refrigerator or microwave. Preheat oven to 450°. Cover and bake for 20 to 30 minutes. Top with desired toppings, such as green onions, Cheddar cheese or sour cream.

FREEZE
up to 6 months
(3 months if using frozen meat.)

Mock Filet Mignon

1 1/2 lbs. lean ground beef
2 C. cooked rice
1 medium onion, minced
1 T. Worcestershire sauce

1 tsp. salt
1/2 tsp. pepper
1/4 tsp. garlic powder
6 strips bacon

In a medium mixing bowl, combine ground beef, cooked rice, onions, Worcestershire sauce, salt, pepper and garlic powder. Mix thoroughly. Shape beef mixture into 6 patties and wrap each patty with a strip of bacon, securing with a toothpick. Wrap individually or place side by side in a baking dish to freeze.

To prepare

Thaw in refrigerator or microwave. Preheat oven to 450°. Place patties in an ungreased, shallow baking dish. Bake for 20 to 25 minutes.

FREEZE
up to 6 months
(3 months if using frozen meat.)

Sweet & Sour Pork

3 T. vegetable oil
2 lbs. fresh boneless pork loin,
   cut into 1" cubes
2 carrots, cut diagonally into
   thin slices
1 T. minced garlic
1 green pepper, sliced

1 (20 oz.) can pineapple chunks
   in syrup
1/4 C. brown sugar
1/2 C. vinegar
2 T. soy sauce
3 T. cornstarch

In a large skillet, heat vegetable oil. Brown pork, making sure to fully cook. Add carrots, garlic and green peppers. Continue to sauté until tender. Add pineapple with syrup, brown sugar, vinegar and soy sauce. Bring to a boil. Reduce heat and let simmer for 10 minutes. In a small bowl, whisk cornstarch and 1/4 cup water together and stir into pork mixture. Simmer a few minutes to thicken. Remove from heat and let cool. Transfer to a casserole dish or freezer bag. Freeze.

To prepare

Heat frozen pork gently over stovetop, stirring occasionally. Serve over rice.

FREEZE
up to 6 months.

Chicken Paprika

1 tsp. salt	2 medium yellow onions, sliced
2 T. paprika	1 green pepper, chopped
1/2 tsp. pepper	6 whole cloves garlic, halved
3 T. olive oil	1/2 C. chicken broth, canned
2 lbs. fresh boneless, skinless	or prepared with bouillon
chicken breast, trimmed of fat	

In a small bowl, combine salt, paprika and pepper. Dust mixture over chicken. In a large skillet, heat olive oil. Brown chicken in oil, cooking 8 to 10 minutes on each side. Remove chicken from skillet and arrange in a greased 9x13" pan. In the same skillet, sauté onions, green peppers and garlic until tender. Add chicken broth and simmer for 10 minutes. Pour over chicken, cover and freeze.

To prepare

1 large tomato, halved and sliced thin

Thaw in refrigerator or microwave. Preheat oven to 350°. Top chicken with slices of tomato. Cover and bake for 30 to 35 minutes. Remove cover and bake an additional 10 minutes.

FREEZE
up to 6 months.

Curried Chicken
or Turkey

1/4 C. vegetable oil	3 T. flour
1 medium onion, chopped	2 C. chicken broth, canned or
2 C. diced and peeled apples	prepared with bouillon
2 tsp. curry powder	4 C. cooked cubed chicken or
	turkey

In a large skillet, heat vegetable oil and sauté onions and apples until softened and beginning to brown. Add curry powder and cook a few minutes longer. Stir in flour to form a paste. Add chicken broth and simmer, allowing sauce to thicken. Stir in cooked chicken or turkey and heat thoroughly. Remove from heat and cool. Transfer to a freezer bag or casserole dish. Cover and freeze.

To prepare

1 T. lemon juice	1/2 C. half n' half

In a large saucepan, heat frozen chicken or turkey over stovetop. Gently stir in lemon juice and half n' half. If desired, serve over cooked rice.

FREEZE
up to 6 months
(3 months if using frozen meat.)

96

Chicken á la King

**1 1/2 lbs. chopped chicken
  breast
1/2 C. butter
1 red bell pepper, chopped
8 oz. sliced fresh mushrooms**

**1 C. frozen peas
1 C. chicken broth, canned or
  prepared with bouillon
1 (10 oz.) can cream of chicken
  soup**

In a large skillet, brown chicken in butter, making sure to fully cook. Add red peppers and mushrooms and continue to sauté until tender. Stir in peas, chicken broth and cream of chicken soup. Remove from heat and let cool. Transfer to a freezer bag or casserole dish. Cover and freeze.

To prepare

In a large skillet, heat frozen chicken over stovetop. If desired, serve with biscuits, pasta or cornbread.

**FREEZE
up to 3 months.**

Chicken Tostadas or Tacos

2 1/2 C. cooked cubed chicken
1 (15 oz.) can kidney beans,
    drained
1 T. vegetable oil
1 red pepper, sliced
1 medium onion, sliced

1 1/2 tsp. chili powder
1/2 tsp. oregano
1/2 tsp. ground cumin
1 (10 oz.) can diced tomatoes
    with green chilies, drained

In a medium bowl, toss together chicken and drained kidney beans. Set aside. In a medium skillet, heat vegetable oil. Add peppers and onions and sauté over high heat until browned. Add chili powder, oregano and ground cumin. Sauté for an additional minute. Stir in drained tomatoes with green chilies and bring to a boil. Let simmer for about 5 minutes. Add chicken and beans to skillet, stirring to combine. Allow to cool and transfer to a freezer bag for freezing.

To prepare

Thaw in refrigerator or microwave. In a large skillet, heat chicken over stovetop. Serve as tacos or tostadas with cheese, lettuce, tomato and salsa.

FREEZE
up to 6 months
(3 months if using frozen meat.)

Chicken Pasta Primavera

1 T. vegetable oil	2 tsp. dried basil
1/2 medium red onion, sliced	1 T. dried parsley flakes
1 T. chopped garlic	2 C. cooked cubed or sliced chicken
1 large carrot, sliced	4 C. cooked small macaroni
1 red pepper, sliced	shells or small sized penne
1 (28 oz.) can diced tomatoes	1 C. shredded mozzarella cheese
in juice	1/3 C. grated Parmesan cheese

In a large skillet, heat oil and sauté onions, garlic, carrots and red peppers until onions are tender. Add tomatoes with juice and bring to a boil. Remove from heat and stir in basil, parsley flakes and cooked chicken. Toss together with cooked pasta. Transfer to a greased 2 1/2-quart casserole dish and top with mozzarella and Parmesan cheese. Cover and freeze.

To prepare

Thaw in refrigerator or microwave. Preheat oven to 350°. Cover and bake for 35 to 40 minutes. Remove cover and bake an additional 10 minutes.

FREEZE
up to 6 months
(3 months if using frozen meat.)

Philly Beef Sandwiches

2 T. butter
1 1/2 lbs. fresh beef sirloin steak,
    cut into thin strips

1 medium onion, sliced thin
1 large green pepper, sliced thin
2 beef bouillon cubes

In a large skillet, heat butter. Sauté beef over high heat until browned and fully cooked. Add onions and green peppers. Cook until tender. Add 1/4 cup water and beef bouillon cubes, stirring to dissolve the cubes. Cover and let simmer for 10 to 15 minutes. Allow to cool before transferring to freezer bags to freeze.

To prepare

Hoagie sandwich buns

Mozzarella cheese slices

Thaw in refrigerator or microwave. Heat beef and vegetables over stovetop. Place over buttered hoagie sandwiches. Top with a slice of mozzarella cheese and cook under broiler until cheese is bubbly and just starting to brown.

FREEZE
up to 6 months.

Wild Rice & Mushroom Chicken Bake

1 (6 oz.) pkg. Uncle Ben's
    long grain and wild rice mix
4 (5 to 6 oz. each) boneless
    chicken breasts

3 T. butter
1 medium red pepper, chopped
1 (4 oz.) can sliced mushrooms,
    drained

Prepare rice according to package directions. In a medium skillet, sauté chicken in butter over medium heat, roughly 8 to 10 minutes on each side. Set aside. Reserve butter in pan and sauté red peppers until tender. Stir in drained mushrooms. Mix peppers and mushrooms with rice. Place chicken breast in a greased 1 1/2-quart casserole dish and top with rice mixture.

To prepare

Thaw in refrigerator or microwave. Preheat oven to 350°. Cover and bake for 40 to 45 minutes.

FREEZE
up to 6 months
(3 months if using frozen meat.)

Dilled Ham over Rice

4 C. ham, cut into long thin
    strips
2 T. butter
2 stalks celery, sliced
1 medium onion, sliced
1 (4 oz.) can sliced mushrooms,
    drained

1 (10 oz.) can cream of chicken
    soup
1/2 C. milk
2 tsp. prepared mustard
2 tsp. dried dill
1/2 C. sour cream

In a medium skillet, sauté ham in butter until lightly browned. Add celery, onions and drained mushrooms and cook until tender. Add cream of chicken soup, milk, mustard and dill and thoroughly heat. Remove from heat and stir in sour cream. Allow to cool before transferring to a freezer bag to freeze.

To prepare

Thaw in refrigerator or microwave. Heat in double boiler or gently over stovetop, stirring constantly. If desired, serve over rice or noodles.

FREEZE
up to 3 months.

Creamy Crock Pot Chicken & Beef

6 (4 to 5 oz. each) boneless
   skinless chicken breasts
6 strips bacon
1 (2 1/2 oz.) pkg. thinly sliced
   dried beef

1/4 C. flour
1 (10 oz.) can cream of mushroom
   soup
1/4 C. sour cream
1/4 C. milk

Fold chicken breasts in half and wrap a strip of bacon around each, securing with a toothpick. Coarsely chop the dried beef. In a medium mixing bowl, combine dried beef with flour, cream of mushroom soup, sour cream and milk. Place chicken in a freezer bag and cover with soup mixture, making sure to mix well.

To prepare

Thaw in refrigerator or microwave. Empty chicken into a slow cooker. Cook on low for 8 to 9 hours. If desired, serve over noodles or rice.

FREEZE
up to 3 months.

103

Pepper Beef Goulash

1/4 C. vegetable oil
2 lbs. beef stew meat
1 (6 oz.) can tomato paste
1 env. Sloppy Joe seasoning

2 stalks celery, chopped
1 large green pepper, chopped
2 T. cider vinegar

In a large skillet, heat vegetable oil and brown beef stew meat. Add 1/2 cup water, tomato paste, Sloppy Joe seasoning, celery, green peppers and cider vinegar. Cook just enough to heat through. Allow to cool before transferring to a large freezer bag to freeze.

To prepare

Thaw in refrigerator or microwave. Empty beef into a slow cooker. Cook on low for 8 to 9 hours. If desired, serve over noodles or rice.

FREEZE
up to 6 months
(3 months if using frozen meat.)

Desserts

Basic Pie Crust

Makes 1 pie crust

1 C. vegetable shortening   **1 tsp. sugar**
2 1/2 C. flour   **1/3 C. plus 1 T. ice water**
1 tsp. salt

In a medium bowl, cut vegetable shortening into flour, salt and sugar using a pastry blender, until the mixture resembles fine crumbs with a few pea-size crumbs remaining. Add ice water and cut in, using the side of a rubber spatula, until the dough begins to form small balls. Press the dough together against the sides of the bowl. If the dough sticks to the bowl, add an extra tablespoon of water. If the dough is wet or sticky, add an extra tablespoon of flour. Divide the dough in half. Roll each half into a ball and press to make disks. Wrap in plastic and let chill in refrigerator for at least 1 hour before freezing.

To prepare

Let the crust thaw completely before rolling out.

FREEZE
up to 6 months.

106

Peach Pecan Crisp

Makes 4 to 6 servings

4 C. sliced peaches, fresh or frozen	2/3 C. sugar
1/3 C. honey	1/4 tsp. salt
1 C. chopped pecans	5 T. butter, melted
2/3 C. flour	

Lightly grease a 9x13" baking dish. Layer sliced peaches across the bottom and drizzle with honey and chopped pecans. If using frozen peaches, it is only necessary to thaw them enough that they can be broken up and layered. Frozen peaches will preserve better if they are not fully thawed and then refrozen. In a medium bowl, combine flour, sugar and salt. Pour melted butter over the top. With the side of a spatula or fork, use a cutting motion to combine until the mixture resembles pea-size crumbs. Sprinkle topping over peaches. Cover and freeze.

To prepare

Preheat oven to 350°. Uncover and bake frozen peach crisp for 60 minutes.

FREEZE
up to 6 months.

107

Freezer Carrot Cake

Makes 1 cake

2 C. flour	1 C. vegetable oil
2 C. sugar	4 eggs
1 tsp. baking powder	3 C. (about 1 lb.) finely shredded
1 tsp. baking soda	carrots
1 tsp. salt	3/4 C. chopped walnuts
1 tsp. cinnamon	

Preheat oven to 325°. In a medium bowl, whisk together flour, sugar, baking powder, baking soda, salt and cinnamon. In a mixing bowl, combine vegetable oil, eggs and shredded carrots and beat until combined. Add walnuts and dry ingredients to mixer and beat at medium speed for 2 minutes. Spread batter into a greased 9x13" baking pan or two 9" rounds. Bake for 35 to 45 minutes. Allow to cool before frosting.

Cream Cheese Icing

6 oz. cream cheese, softened	2 C. powdered sugar
4 T. butter or margarine	1/2 C. chopped walnuts
1 tsp. vanilla	

In a medium mixing bowl, combine cream cheese and butter. Beat at high speed until combined. Add vanilla and powdered sugar. Beat at medium high speed until light and fluffy, about 2 to 4 minutes. Ice tops of cakes only. Sprinkle frosting with chopped walnuts. Cover cake and freeze.

FREEZE
up to 6 months.

To prepare

Let cake thaw until softened. Cut into slices to serve.

Frozen Strawberry Margarita Dessert

Makes 8 to 10 servings

1 1/4 C. finely crushed pretzels
1/4 C. sugar
1/2 C. butter, melted
1 (14 oz.) can sweetened
    condensed milk
1/4 C. lime juice

1/4 C. orange juice
1 (10 oz.) pkg. frozen strawberries
    in syrup, thawed
1 C. heavy whipping cream,
    whipped

In a small bowl, combine crushed pretzels, sugar and melted butter. Press pretzel mixture into the bottom of an ungreased 10" springform pan and chill in refrigerator. In a large mixing bowl, combine sweetened condensed milk, lime juice and orange juice and beat until smooth. Add strawberries with syrup and mix until combined. Fold in whipped cream and pour over chilled pretzel crust. Cover and freeze.

To prepare

Let cake thaw until softened. Cut into slices to serve.

FREEZE
up to 3 months.

Frozen Pumpkin Pie

Makes 8 servings

1 1/2 C. gingersnap cookie
    crumbs
1/4 C. butter, melted
1 C. canned pumpkin
1/4 C. brown sugar
1/4 tsp. salt

1 tsp. pumpkin pie spice
1 (4 oz.) container frozen
    whipped topping, thawed
2 C. butter pecan ice cream,
    softened

Preheat oven to 350°. Combine cookie crumbs and melted butter in a small bowl. Press onto bottom and up sides of a 9" pie plate and bake for 8 minutes. Let cool completely. In a medium bowl, mix canned pumpkin, brown sugar, salt and pumpkin pie spice. Fold in whipped topping until blended. Fold in softened ice cream to marble. Place in cooled crust and freeze for 3 hours. When firm, cover and return to freezer.

To prepare

Remove from freezer 15 minutes prior to serving time. Cut into slices to serve.

FREEZE
up to 3 months.

Coffee Almond Tart

Makes 8 servings

18 chocolate sandwich cookies, crushed	**1 qt. coffee ice cream, slightly softened**
3 T. butter, melted	**1/3 C. sliced almonds, toasted***

In a medium bowl, combine crushed cookies and melted butter and press on bottom and up sides of a 9" pie plate. Freeze for 15 minutes or until firm. Spread softened ice cream gently and evenly over crust. Sprinkle with toasted almonds. Freeze at least 3 hours or until firm. When firm, cover and return to freezer.

* To toast, place almonds in a single layer on a baking sheet. Bake at 350° for approximately 10 minutes or until nuts are golden brown.

To prepare

1 C. hot fudge sauce

Remove torte from freezer 10 minutes before serving. Serve with hot fudge sauce.

FREEZE
up to 6 months.

111

Lemonade
Ice Cream Pie

Makes 8 servings

4 C. vanilla ice cream, softened   **1 (9") graham cracker crust**
1 (6 oz.) can frozen lemonade
     concentrate, thawed

In a medium bowl, mix softened ice cream and thawed lemonade concentrate. Immediately spoon mixture into graham cracker crust. Freeze at least 4 hours or until firm.

Variations

Try your own favorite combinations of ice cream and frozen juice concentrate.

To prepare

Let stand at room temperature for a few minutes before cutting and serving.

FREEZE
up to 6 months.

Caramel Apple Cake

Makes 1 cake

1 3/4 C. flour	1 tsp. vanilla
1 1/2 C. brown sugar	3/4 C. butter, softened
1 1/2 tsp. cinnamon	3 eggs
1/2 tsp. salt	1 1/2 C. (about 2 medium) apples,
1/2 tsp. baking powder	peeled and finely chopped
1/2 tsp. baking soda	1 C. chopped pecans

Preheat oven to 350°. Grease only the bottom of 9x13" pan and set aside. In a large mixing bowl, combine flour, brown sugar, cinnamon, salt, baking powder, baking soda, vanilla, butter and eggs. Beat on medium speed until batter is smooth, about 2 to 3 minutes. Stir in apples and pecans by hand. Pour batter into prepared pan. Bake for 30 to 40 minutes or until toothpick inserted in center comes out clean. Cool completely on wire rack before frosting.

Caramel Frosting

1/2 C. butter	1 tsp. vanilla
1 C. brown sugar	3 to 4 C. powdered
1/4 C. milk	sugar, sifted

In a large saucepan, melt butter and add brown sugar. Bring to a boil, stirring frequently. Boil and stir for 1 minute until thickened. Remove from heat and add milk. Beat with wire whisk until smooth. Add vanilla and beat again. Add enough powdered sugar until frosting reaches desired spreading consistency. Pour frosting over cake and spread to cover. Let cool completely before freezing.

To prepare

Let cake thaw until softened. Cut into slices to serve.

FREEZE
up to 6 months.

Decadent Ice Cream Cake

Makes 1 cake

2 1/4 C. crumbled macaroons, divided
3 C. chocolate ice cream, slightly softened
5 Heath bars, coarsely chopped, divided

4 T. chocolate syrup, divided
3 T. Kahlua liquor, divided
3 C. vanilla ice cream, slightly softened

Layer the bottom of an 8" springform pan with 1 1/4 cups crumbled macaroons. Spread softened chocolate ice cream evenly over the macaroons. Spread 4 (or 4/5) of the crushed Heath bars over the ice cream. Drizzle 3 tablespoons chocolate syrup and 2 tablespoons Kahlua over chocolate ice cream. Cover with remaining 1 cup macaroons. Top evenly with softened vanilla ice cream. Sprinkle remaining crushed Heath bars over vanilla ice cream. Drizzle with remaining chocolate syrup and Kahlua. Cover and freeze for at least 8 hours or overnight.

Variations

May use other cookies or crumbs in place of macaroons.

FREEZE
up to 6 months.

To prepare

Let stand at room temperature for a few minutes before cutting and serving.

Creamy Peanut Dessert

1 1/2 C. graham cracker crumbs	1 (8 oz.) pkg. cream cheese, softened
1/2 C. chopped salted peanuts	1/2 C. sugar
1/4 C. butter, melted	2 tsp. vanilla
1/2 C. plus 2 T. peanut butter, divided	1 (16 oz.) container frozen whipped topping, thawed
	4 T. chocolate syrup

In a small mixing bowl, combine graham cracker crumbs, chopped peanuts, melted butter and 2 tablespoons peanut butter. Mix well. Press into a greased 9x13" pan, reserving 1/2 cup of crumb mixture for topping. Refrigerate for 30 minutes to allow to set. Meanwhile, in a mixing bowl, beat cream cheese, remaining 1/2 cup peanut butter, sugar and vanilla until smooth. Fold in whipped topping and spoon over crust. Drizzle chocolate syrup over top and sprinkle with reserved crumb mixture. Cover and freeze until ready to serve.

To prepare

Let stand at room temperature for a few minutes before cutting and serving.

FREEZE
up to 3 months.

Sherbet Cookie Dessert

2 qts. strawberry sherbet ice cream, softened
1/3 C. powdered sugar
2 C. frozen whipped topping, thawed

15 Oreo cookies, broken into pieces
3/4 C. sliced almonds, toasted*

Spread sherbet over the bottom of a 9x13" pan. Place in freezer for 10 minutes to set. In a medium mixing bowl, combine powdered sugar and whipped topping. Fold in Oreo cookie pieces and toasted almonds. Spread mixture over sherbet in pan. Cover and return to freezer.

* To toast, place almonds in a single layer on a baking sheet. Bake at 350° for approximately 10 minutes or until nuts are golden brown.

To prepare

Let stand at room temperature for a few minutes before cutting and serving.

FREEZE
up to 3 months.

Chocolate Sundae Pie

4 oz. cream cheese, softened
1/2 C. sweetened condensed
   milk
4 tsp. unsweetened cocoa
   powder
1 (8 oz.) container frozen
   whipped topping, thawed

1 (9") Oreo cookie crumb
   crust
1/2 C. chocolate syrup
1/2 C. chopped pecans

In a medium mixing bowl, beat cream cheese until smooth. Add sweetened condensed milk and cocoa powder, beating again until smooth. Fold in the whipped topping. Turn mixture out into Oreo cookie crust. Drizzle chocolate syrup over top and sprinkle with chopped pecans. Cover and freeze.

To prepare

Let stand at room temperature for a few minutes before cutting and serving.

FREEZE
up to 3 months.

German Chocolate Cream Pie

4 oz. German sweet chocolate
1/3 C. half n' half
4 oz. cream cheese, softened
1/4 C. sugar

1 (8 oz.) container frozen whipped topping, thawed
1 (9") graham cracker crust

In a double boiler, melt German sweet chocolate with half n' half, stirring until smooth and just melted. In a mixing bowl, beat cream cheese and sugar until smooth. Stir in chocolate mixture until well blended. Fold in whipped topping and spoon into crust. Cover and freeze until ready to serve.

To prepare

Let stand at room temperature for a few minutes before cutting and serving.

FREEZE
up to 3 months.

118

Frosty Blueberry Dessert

1 (21 oz.) can blueberry pie
    filling
1 (21 oz.) can evaporated milk
1/4 C. fresh lemon juice

1/2 tsp. almond extract
1 (8 oz.) container frozen
    whipped topping, thawed

In a medium mixing bowl, combine pie filling, evaporated milk, lemon juice and almond extract, stirring until well blended. Fold in whipped topping. Spread mixture into a greased 7x11" pan. Cover and freeze.

To prepare

Let stand at room temperature for a few minutes before cutting and serving.

FREEZE
up to 3 months.

119

Chocolate Chip Cookie Ice Cream Cake

Makes 1 (9") cake

**1 (18 oz.) pkg. small chocolate
   chip cookies
1/4 C. margarine, melted**

**3/4 C. hot fudge topping
2 qts. vanilla ice cream, divided**

In a large bowl, crush half of the cookies into small crumbs. Add melted margarine and stir to combine. Press mixture into the bottom of a 9" springform pan or pie plate. Line the remaining whole cookies around the edge of the pan, standing against the side. Spread fudge topping over crust. Freeze for 15 minutes. Meanwhile, soften 1 quart ice cream at room temperature or in microwave. After crust has chilled, spread softened ice cream over fudge and freeze an additional 30 minutes. Scoop remaining quart of ice cream into balls with a melon-balling tool and arrange evenly over spread ice cream layer. Freeze 4 hours until firm or overnight.

To prepare

**1/4 C. hot fudge topping
1 C. whipped cream**

12 cherries

Let stand at room temperature a few minutes before serving. Garnish with fudge topping, whipped cream and cherries.

**FREEZE
up to 3 months.**

Index

Veggies & Sides

Soups

Casseroles

Main Dishes

Desserts